The techniques for applying wallpaper
are demonstrated on pages 56-65 — and the
special handling required for a dormered
room is explained on page 65.

Walls

Square foot for square foot, walls are the largest single feature the designer has to consider in decorating a room. Their basic functions — to enclose and define space, to create areas of privacy — remain constants. But as decorative elements, walls can vary enormously, from being so understated as to go virtually unnoticed, to becoming dramatic accents in their own right.

With painted walls, for example, flat white is the most frequent choice from coast to coast, so familiar that we scarcely notice it. But deeper, brighter colors, lustrous finishes, dramatic textures, stenciling and even one-of-a-kind murals are tempting options that deserve consideration. So, too, wood moldings — affixed at the base of the wall, at chair-rail height, just below the ceiling, and around windows and doors — are attractive refinements. Such trim strips used to be custom-crafted and therefore costly, but now, thanks to the miracles of modern millworking, they are available to the home decorator in a wide range of stock sizes and silhouettes, and at nominal expense.

Pattern is another way to make something special out of a room's walls. Wallpapers are the most familiar route to patterning, and they come in a range of colors, motifs, finishes and qualities to satisfy almost anyone's imagination. But in situations where a softer, more luxurious look or a sound-muffling effect is wanted, fabric mounted on rods or stapled directly to the wall surface can do an even better job. Lastly, walls sheathed partially or fully with wood panels or planking become attention-getters. Wood surfacing usually represents a substantial investment in time and money, but the rewards in terms of creating a room permanently rich in warmth and character are great.

The selection of handsome interiors shown on the next 10 pages will give you an idea of the many venturesome ways in which walls can gain decorative appeal. Starting on page 16, you will learn about the professional techniques that can turn your imaginings into reality.

Compounds of naturally colored marble dust in three different hues, mixed with slaked lime and glue, were troweled over plaster to create the unusual wall and ceiling surfaces shown here. A second troweling, done just before the first coat dried, refined the texture and revealed variegated shades of ingrained color. Beeswax, hand-rubbed into the wall surfaces, gives them a sheen that — in combination with highly polished stone floors, high-gloss enameled furniture and a generous expanse of mirrors — produces a luminous quality in these rooms.

A *trompe l'oeil* mural, rich with Old World country-kitchen images, becomes a poetic refuge from the high-tech gadgetry of the real kitchen that adjoins it. The mural

was applied over fine-sanded painted walls. Colors were built up in layers, much as in a fine painting, to achieve maximum dimensional effect.

A cotton print of modest scale, used to cover walls, ceiling and bed alike, transforms a child's small bedroom into a very special hideaway. The underlayer of batting on the walls, the dark-colored braid that trims the juncture of walls and ceiling, the coordinated throw pillows — all bespeak careful attention to detail.

Chinese grass cloth, a weave of natural grasses on paper backing, provides a congenial backdrop for a collection of Oriental furniture and artworks. Grass cloth cannot be perfectly matched panel to panel, but its subtle variations become an asset when it sets the stage for wide-ranging wood, ceramic and fabric tones and textures, such as those assembled here.

Using bands of half-round wood molding, the designer of this contemporary dining room turned plain walls into a dominant decorative element. Classic in spirit, the proportion and form of the banding tie closely to surroundings: 7-inch stair risers provide the module for spacing the millwork, and the half-round profile finds echoes in cylindrical stair and balcony rails. Recessed lighting spills down the soft-toned walls in a crescendo of dramatic highlights and shadows.

Columns, moldings and mirror bring an air of ceremonial importance to a stark entryway. The columns are made of wooden staves, smooth-sanded and painted in a high-gloss off-white. Half-round molding centered on narrow wood strips is fashioned into simple chair rails; ordinary lumber forms baseboards. Both extend from the pale yellow foreground to the blue-gray area at rear, to provide a unifying horizontal motif that draws the eye from one space to the next.

In a contemporary beach house, rough-sawn cedar tongue-and-groove paneling sharply defines the angles of a spectacular room. For added interest, some sections of

panels are installed on the diagonal, others horizontally. By contrast, walls in the fireplace alcove and halls are clad in low-key white-painted wallboard.

Other Publications:
UNDERSTANDING COMPUTERS
THE ENCHANTED WORLD
THE KODAK LIBRARY OF CREATIVE PHOTOGRAPHY
GREAT MEALS IN MINUTES
THE CIVIL WAR
PLANET EARTH
COLLECTOR'S LIBRARY OF THE CIVIL WAR
THE EPIC OF FLIGHT
THE GOOD COOK
WORLD WAR II
HOME REPAIR AND IMPROVEMENT
THE OLD WEST

*For information on and a full
description of any of the Time-Life Books
series listed above, please write:*
Reader Information
Time-Life Books
541 North Fairbanks Court
Chicago, Illinois 60611

This volume is one of a series that features home decorating projects.

Walls

by the Editors of Time-Life Books

TIME-LIFE BOOKS □ ALEXANDRIA, VIRGINIA

YOUR HOME

THE CONSULTANTS

David A. Bennett Sr. is a union journeyman painter and paperhanger with more than 25 years' experience in his trade. He is especially noted for creating textured wall treatments, several of which appear in this book.

Nancy T. Baker and Cindy B. Fitch are decorative artists who specialize in painted finishes for home interiors. This book features samples of these finishes and the techniques for achieving them. Nancy Baker graduated from the Isabel O'Neil Studio Workshop in New York; Cindy Fitch studied art and interior design at the University of Texas in Austin and at El Centro College in Dallas, Texas.

Robert L. Petersen, a cabinetmaker and woodwork specialist, designs and executes custom wall treatments.

Lowell Wade belongs to the American Society of Interior Designers. A graduate of the Art Institute in Pittsburgh, Pennsylvania, she owns her own decorating studio, Interior Motives, in Alexandria, Virginia.

Frederick L. Wall, a furniture maker and sculptor, is an assistant professor in furniture design at the Corcoran School of Art in Washington, D.C. His work has been featured in many exhibits and publications.

Library of Congress Cataloguing in
Publication Data
Main entry under title:
Walls.

(Your home)
Includes index.
1. Interior walls. 2. Dwellings — Remodeling.
I. Time-Life Books. II. Series.
TH2239.W35 1986   643'.7   85-16555
ISBN 0-8094-5537-4
ISBN 0-8094-5538-2 (lib. bdg.)

CONTENTS

Walls from the inside out

For anyone with an eye for color and decoration, the walls of a room are a standing invitation to imaginative and bold experimentation. But like any artist, the person who sets out to transform walls would do well to understand their nature before plunging into a project, no matter how small or seemingly insignificant it may be.

House walls look as solid as stone. Most, however, are like airplane wings — mere skins nailed to frames, with wires and pipes coursing through. These are wood-frame walls, excellent for repelling weather and dividing interior space. They consist of a skeleton of vertical 2-by-4s, called studs, bounded at top and bottom by horizontal 2-by-4s, called the top plate and the sole plate. Hidden to the eye, these boards provide underlying surfaces for nailing molding and paneling. A foolproof way to locate them is shown on page 19. Windows and doors interrupt the regular rhythm of the studs with their own frameworks, and other patterns of boards are positioned at corners and ceilings. Brick and concrete-block walls, of course, really do resemble stone. Massive and tough, these walls often form the foundation of a house as well as its walls.

No matter what composes its thickness, a wall is invariably covered with a thin finishing veneer. In homes built before the mid-1940s, the veneer is usually plaster. Nowadays, it is more likely to be 4-by-8-foot sheets of wallboard, a chalklike gypsum sandwiched between layers of thick paper. The heads of the nails holding wallboard in place and the seams between individual sheets are covered with a pasty substance called joint compound.

Eventually, wear, tear and the natural settling of a house onto its foundation can cause both wallboard and plaster to deteriorate: Cracks appear mysteriously, nailheads pop, seams pull apart and holes are made accidentally. Recognizing and repairing such surface damage (*pages 22-23*) is prerequisite to beginning most of the projects in this book.

Wallboard on Studs: An Interior Wall

For most interior walls the main components are studs and wallboard. The studs, 2-by-4 boards set at regular intervals, are generally 16 inches apart, but can be as far apart as 24 inches. They are braced by short 2-by-4 blocks called firestops positioned halfway between the floor and ceiling to cut off dangerous updrafts should the house catch on fire.

Beneath the studs is a horizontal 2-by-4 called a sole plate. Above the studs is a top plate, made in most cases of two 2-by-4s. The top plate supports the ceiling joists, normally 2-by-10 boards spaced 16 inches apart.

Extra studs, called king studs, are installed at door openings. Nailed to them are jack studs and an assemblage called a header, usually 2-by-6s sandwiching a ½-inch sheet of plywood. Atop the header, short 2-by-4s, called cripple studs, maintain the stud's regular spacing. Utilities run inside the walls; for clues to their routes, look for heating registers and electric outlets, and be mindful of the locations of bathrooms and kitchens.

Covering all is a skin of wallboard nailed to the studs. Joint compound — reinforced by paper tape at seams — smooths over depressions and gaps.

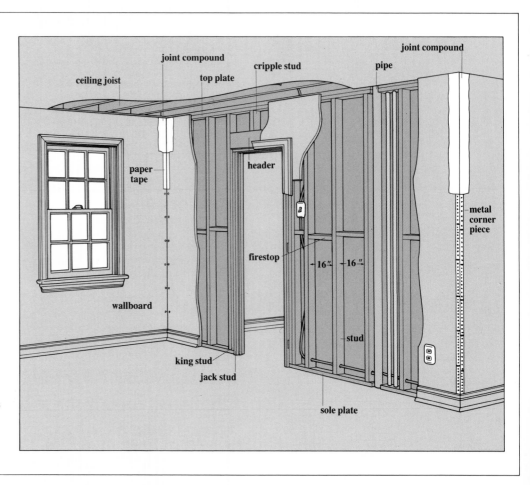

16

Wallboard on Studs: An Exterior Wall

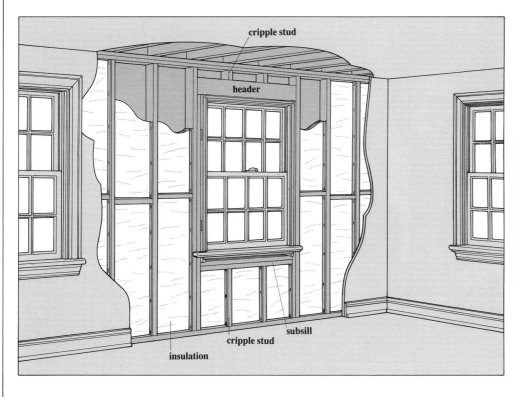

Slight differences distinguish an exterior wood-frame wall from an interior one. Added is insulation, placed between the studs. Subtracted are supply pipes and heating ducts — cold air can freeze the former and rob heat from the latter. Furthermore, it is windows, not doors, that interrupt exterior walls. The framing for windows mimics that for doors, but with a bottom horizontal 2-by-4 called a subsill and 2-by-4 cripple studs below it that align with cripple studs over the header.

Corner Configurations

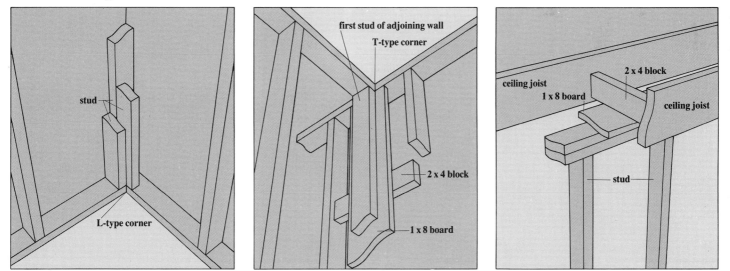

To make solid corners that provide essential nailing surfaces, carpenters arrange various wood pieces in special ways. At an L-type intersection, carpenters nail together three studs in the pattern shown above, at left; the configuration offers at least 1½ inches of nailing surface on each side, or a little less than 1 inch after wallboard is installed. At a T-type intersection (above, center), carpenters nail 2-by-4 blocks every 2 feet between the studs, set back ¾ inch from the stud edges. A 1-by-8 board is nailed to the blocks; the first stud of the adjoining wall is then nailed to the 1-by-8. Where a wall runs parallel to ceiling joists (above, right), carpenters use the same technique. But where a wall runs perpendicular to joists, they merely nail the top plate to the joist bottoms.

Wallboard over Masonry

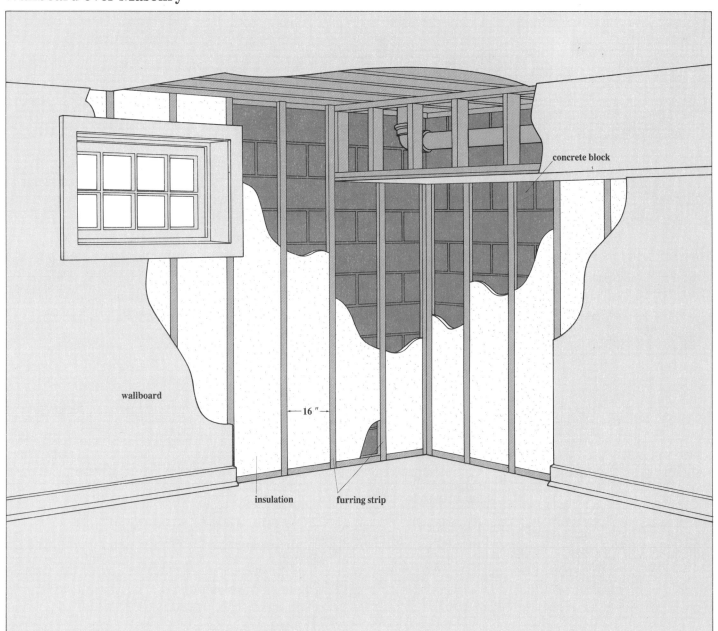

concrete block

wallboard

— 16 ″ —

insulation   furring strip

Before walls of poured concrete, brick, cinder block or, as here, concrete block are covered with wallboard, they first are framed by 1-by-3 wood strips, called furring. The furring is set vertically on the wall at 16-inch intervals beginning from the corners — where pairs of strips meet at right angles. Furring can be fastened to masonry with masonry nails, adhesive or both. Horizontal strips often are added at floor and ceiling.

Ducts or pipes thicker than ¾ inch or so can be concealed by enclosing them in boxlike structures that consist of 2-by-3s or 2-by-4s put together like wood-frame walls. These structures are supported by nails driven into ceiling joists and by bolts anchored to the wall.

On exterior walls, insulation — here, a rigid form type — is placed between furring strips. Then wallboard is nailed to the strips just as it is nailed to the studs of a wood-frame wall.

Plaster over Masonry and Wood

With masonry as a base — here, an exterior brick wall of a type commonly found in homes built before the mid-1940s — plaster is usually applied in two coats.

But to cover a wood-frame wall, three coats are the norm. To provide strong anchorage for the first of the three coats, strips of rough wood lath often are nailed horizontally to the studs, with ¼-inch gaps between them. The first coat of plaster oozes through the lath, covers the backs of the strips, dries and holds fast. While it is still soft, the base coat on lath is lined with grooves to give successive coats a surface they can bond to.

In recent times, wood lath has been replaced by gypsum lath, which comes in the form of rigid sheets similar to wallboard, but much smaller in size. At corners and ceilings — and sometimes at corners of windows and doors — wood or gypsum lath may be reinforced with strips of metal lath, galvanized-steel mesh through which nails and screws can easily be driven.

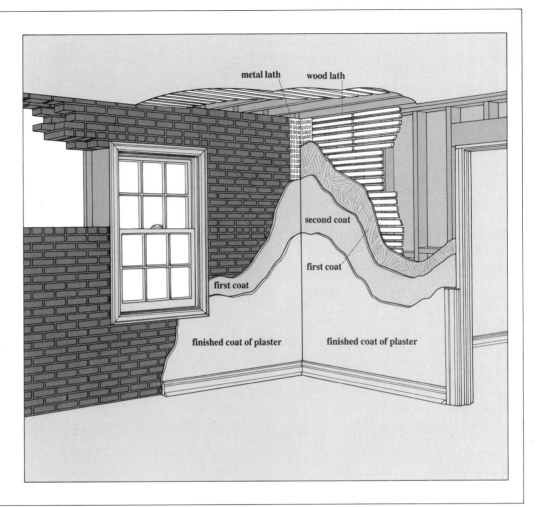

metal lath   wood lath

second coat

first coat

first coat

finished coat of plaster   finished coat of plaster

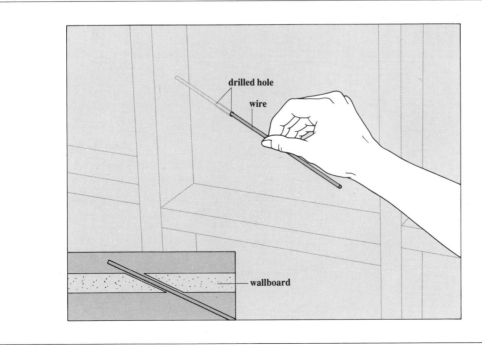

drilled hole

wire

wallboard

Locating an Unseen Stud

A quick and easy way to locate a stud or other nailing surface requires only a drill and a stiff wire. First, tap the wall with your knuckle: A low-pitched, hollow sound indicates the space between studs; a high-pitched, solid sound indicates a stud.

To confirm the stud's exact location, drill a small hole several inches away from and slanted toward where you tapped the wall. Insert the wire through the hole (inset) until it hits the stud's side — in an exterior wall you are likely to encounter insulation, but keep pushing. When the wire hits wood, grip it just where it enters the hole, extract it and position it at the same angle outside the wallboard. The tip of the wire should now indicate the stud's edge; measure ¾ inch farther to find the stud's center. Test your results by driving a small nail there. To locate another point higher or lower on the same stud, use a level held vertical. To locate adjacent studs, set a level on a yardstick and measure 16 inches to either side.

Preparing the surface for redecoration

Before you apply a single stroke with paintbrush or roller, walls and ceilings should be clean and smooth; woodwork should have its original contours. Each room should also be stripped of unnecessary impediments. Allowing enough time to reach both goals is your best insurance that the painting will go efficiently and safely.

● *Treating wallpaper.* Clean, tight paper can be painted over unless coated with vinyl, which rejects paint. Removing paper *(page 57)* is wiser; paint softens wallpaper paste, loosening the paper.

● *Cleaning walls.* Painted wallboard or plaster walls in good condition require little more than dusting, followed by a thorough wash with an abrasive cleanser. Use a sponge soaked in mineral spirits for excessively greasy spots, blot them dry and wash them with cleanser. Simply dust ceilings and unpainted wallboard. Coat unfinished surfaces with primer-sealer.

● *Handling old paint.* Leave old paint that adheres tightly. If a small portion of a painted surface is flaking, clear it with a putty knife *(opposite);* if old paint is peeling badly, strip it off with chemicals or —

where damaged areas are large — buy or rent a heat gun, an electric hot-air paint-removal tool *(top row, center).*

● *Patching.* The material for patching holes and cracks must match the job at hand. Vinyl spackling compound suits wallboard or plaster cracks and holes up to 1 inch across. For openings 1 to 4 inches in diameter, patching plaster is best. Wallboard holes larger than 4 inches across require a patch of new wallboard. Wallboard joint cement is used to fill open wallboard joints, nail dimples and shallow dents; unlike spackle, the cement will not crumble when spread paper-thin.

After it has dried, sand spackle or plaster with fine (150-grit) paper. Smooth dried wallboard joint cement with a wet sponge; it will disintegrate if sanded. No matter what patching material is used, all repaired areas should be coated with a pigmented primer-sealer. If you are repainting with a light-colored paint, prime the patch with the color you will use for the finish coat. If you plan to enamel the surface, use pigmented shellac.

● *Preparing woodwork.* If you do not plan to strip it, wash painted woodwork

with detergent. Sand new or stripped woodwork with fine (150-grit) sandpaper. After the sanding, dust it with a tack rag and apply a pigmented primer-sealer.

● *Clearing the room.* Move any portable furnishings, such as table lamps, end tables and small chairs, to other rooms. Group heavy furniture in the center of the room underneath protective dropcloths. Clear plastic sheets, available at hardware stores, make moistureproof dropcloths, but fabric sheets can be substituted. Cover the floor or carpeting too. Tape the dropcloths together to prevent them from separating while you work.

Curtains, shades, pictures and other wall-hung items should be taken down along with their rods or brackets. Use masking tape or peel-off film, sold at paint stores in penlike applicators, to protect hardware that is not easily removed: doorknobs, hinges and the like.

● *Turning off electricity.* After shutting off the room's electricity at the circuit box, remove the cover plates from electric outlets and wall switches. Loosen light fixtures and cover them with plastic bags or newspaper, or remove entirely.

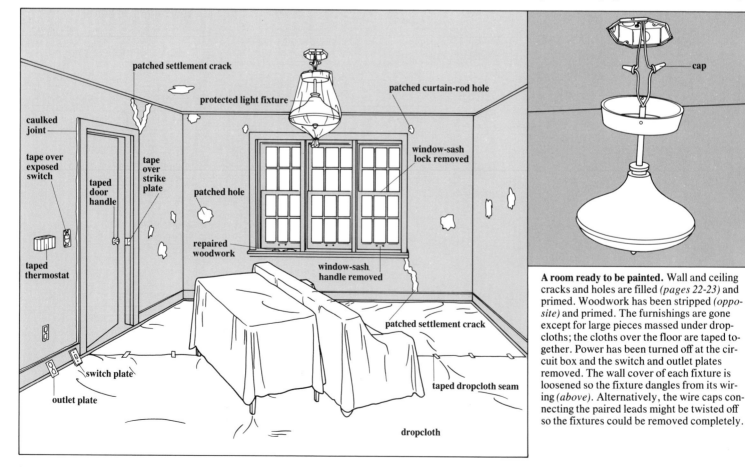

A room ready to be painted. Wall and ceiling cracks and holes are filled *(pages 22-23)* and primed. Woodwork has been stripped *(opposite)* and primed. The furnishings are gone except for large pieces massed under dropcloths; the cloths over the floor are taped together. Power has been turned off at the circuit box and the switch and outlet plates removed. The wall cover of each fixture is loosened so the fixture dangles from its wiring *(above).* Alternatively, the wire caps connecting the paired leads might be twisted off so the fixtures could be removed completely.

Scraping Loose Paint

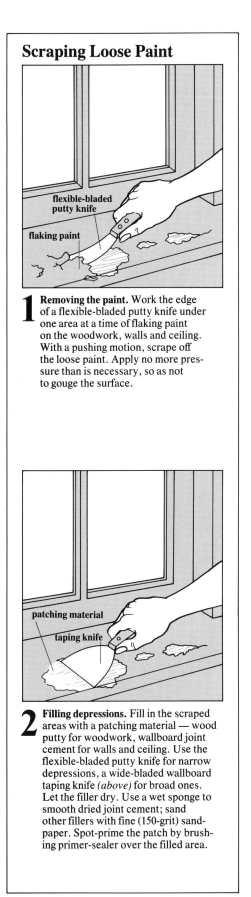

1 Removing the paint. Work the edge of a flexible-bladed putty knife under one area at a time of flaking paint on the woodwork, walls and ceiling. With a pushing motion, scrape off the loose paint. Apply no more pressure than is necessary, so as not to gouge the surface.

2 Filling depressions. Fill in the scraped areas with a patching material — wood putty for woodwork, wallboard joint cement for walls and ceiling. Use the flexible-bladed putty knife for narrow depressions, a wide-bladed wallboard taping knife (above) for broad ones. Let the filler dry. Use a wet sponge to smooth dried joint cement; sand other fillers with fine (150-grit) sandpaper. Spot-prime the patch by brushing primer-sealer over the filled area.

Stripping with Heat

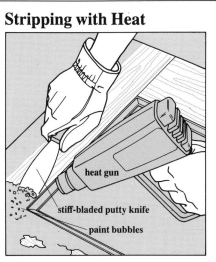

Wear work gloves to protect against burns: The nozzle and paint scrapings can be very hot. Guide the gun with one hand, holding the nozzle 1 or 2 inches from the surface; use a stiff-bladed putty knife in the other hand to scrape off the paint as it softens (above). Alkyd paints bubble when heated (above); latex paints only soften. If all layers are not removed on the first pass, repeat the process.

Sealing Open Joints

To fill gaps between walls and window frames or doorframes, baseboards or ceiling moldings, first fit a tube of all-purpose caulk into a caulking gun. With a utility knife, cut off the tube's tip at a 45° angle. Holding the gun at a 45° angle to the wall, squeeze the trigger and move the tube tip along the gap, creating a uniform caulk bead. To stop the flow of caulk, release the trigger; turn the plunger rod so its teeth point up and pull back the rod.

Removing Paint with Chemical Strippers

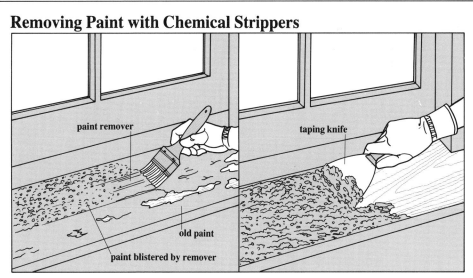

Wearing work gloves, goggles and old clothes, brush on a generous amount of water-washable paste-type paint remover with a clean paintbrush, using short strokes in one direction (above, left). Cover no more than 2 square feet at a time. When the paint begins to wrinkle, peel it off with a stiff-bladed putty knife or a taping knife (above, right). Clean the blade often by wiping it on newspaper. Follow the instructions on the paint-remover label to clean the bare surfaces.

Repairing Small Holes

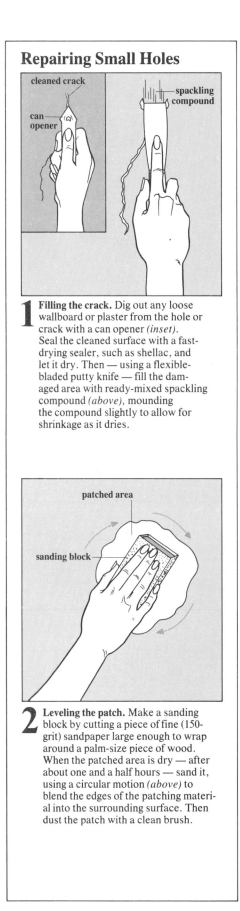

1 Filling the crack. Dig out any loose wallboard or plaster from the hole or crack with a can opener (inset). Seal the cleaned surface with a fast-drying sealer, such as shellac, and let it dry. Then — using a flexible-bladed putty knife — fill the damaged area with ready-mixed spackling compound (above), mounding the compound slightly to allow for shrinkage as it dries.

2 Leveling the patch. Make a sanding block by cutting a piece of fine (150-grit) sandpaper large enough to wrap around a palm-size piece of wood. When the patched area is dry — after about one and a half hours — sand it, using a circular motion (above) to blend the edges of the patching material into the surrounding surface. Then dust the patch with a clean brush.

Repairing Medium-Size Holes in Wallboard

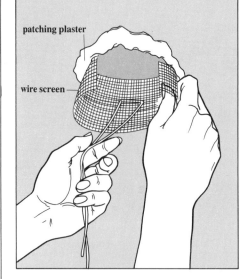

1 Inserting a wire screen. Clean out any loose or torn wallboard from around the hole. With scissors, cut a wire-screen rectangle slightly larger than the hole. Thread a length of string through the wire. Dampen the edges of the hole with water and use a flexible-bladed putty knife to apply patching plaster to the edges. Roll the screen to fit it through the hole (left). Pull the string taut to draw the screen flat against the inside of the hole.

2 Plastering the screen. Place a wood stick across the hole and tie the string to the stick. Dampen the area around the hole. Using a putty knife, plaster over the screen to a level almost flush with the surface. After the plaster has set for a half hour, cut the string and remove it with the stick, thus exposing a spot of bare screen. Dampen the plaster around it and add another plaster coat to bring the patch flush with the surface.

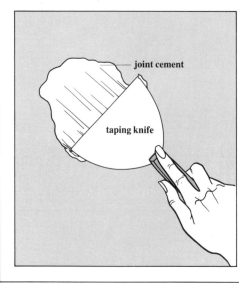

3 Completing the patch. After the second coat of plaster has set for a half hour, cover the patch with a thin layer of wallboard joint cement, using a wide-bladed taping knife (left). Spread the joint cement evenly and smoothly with slow, steady sweeps of the knife. Use the knife to clean away any excess material. Let the patch dry for 24 hours, then smooth it level with the surface, using a wet sponge.

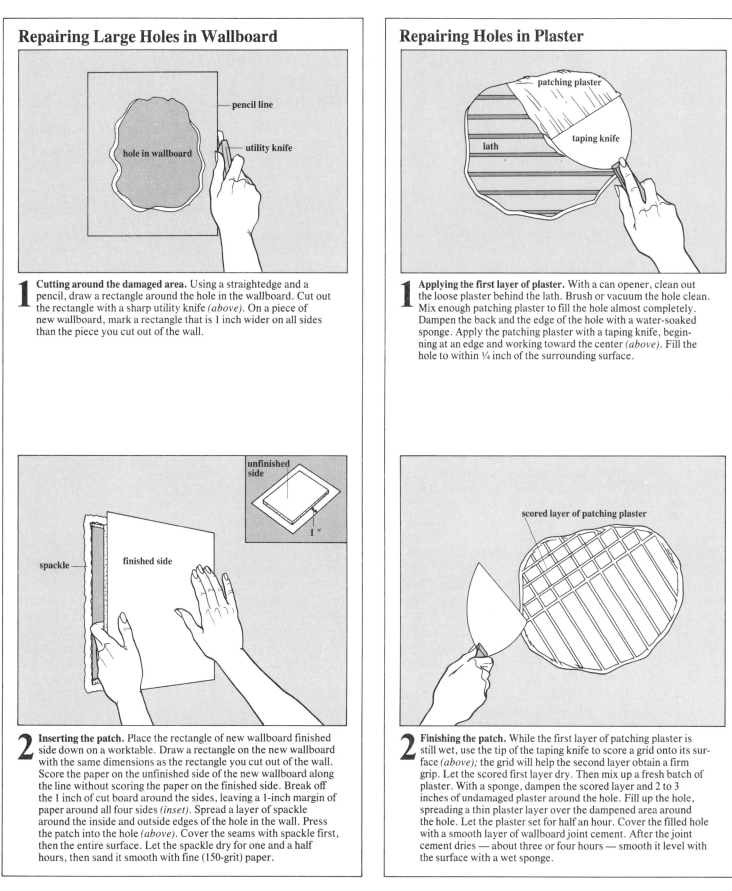

Repairing Large Holes in Wallboard

1 **Cutting around the damaged area.** Using a straightedge and a pencil, draw a rectangle around the hole in the wallboard. Cut out the rectangle with a sharp utility knife *(above)*. On a piece of new wallboard, mark a rectangle that is 1 inch wider on all sides than the piece you cut out of the wall.

2 **Inserting the patch.** Place the rectangle of new wallboard finished side down on a worktable. Draw a rectangle on the new wallboard with the same dimensions as the rectangle you cut out of the wall. Score the paper on the unfinished side of the new wallboard along the line without scoring the paper on the finished side. Break off the 1 inch of cut board around the sides, leaving a 1-inch margin of paper around all four sides *(inset)*. Spread a layer of spackle around the inside and outside edges of the hole in the wall. Press the patch into the hole *(above)*. Cover the seams with spackle first, then the entire surface. Let the spackle dry for one and a half hours, then sand it smooth with fine (150-grit) paper.

Repairing Holes in Plaster

1 **Applying the first layer of plaster.** With a can opener, clean out the loose plaster behind the lath. Brush or vacuum the hole clean. Mix enough patching plaster to fill the hole almost completely. Dampen the back and the edge of the hole with a water-soaked sponge. Apply the patching plaster with a taping knife, beginning at an edge and working toward the center *(above)*. Fill the hole to within ¼ inch of the surrounding surface.

2 **Finishing the patch.** While the first layer of patching plaster is still wet, use the tip of the taping knife to score a grid onto its surface *(above)*; the grid will help the second layer obtain a firm grip. Let the scored first layer dry. Then mix up a fresh batch of plaster. With a sponge, dampen the scored layer and 2 to 3 inches of undamaged plaster around the hole. Fill up the hole, spreading a thin plaster layer over the dampened area around the hole. Let the plaster set for half an hour. Cover the filled hole with a smooth layer of wallboard joint cement. After the joint cement dries — about three or four hours — smooth it level with the surface with a wet sponge.

Decorating
with paint

Used knowledgeably, color is the most effective of decorating tools — and the least expensive, too, when you buy it in a paint can. Even in small doses, fresh colors bring brightness. When lavished across surfaces as dominant as walls, paints can transform rooms, altering the sense of space, disguising architectural faults and dramatizing virtues, creating new moods with color. The rooms on pages 26-27 suggest how.

To pick colors confidently and put them together with flair, you must develop a familiarity with how color works. Visually, color is experienced in three ways. First, color is perceived as hue. Hue refers to the basic color families that blend one into another to form an interrelated circle or wheel (right). Red, blue and yellow constitute the primaries — colors that exist "as is," without mixing — and orange, green and purple the secondaries. Secondary colors are pairs of primaries mixed in equal amounts. The mixing of secondaries and primaries yields the intermediate hues sometimes called tertiaries: red-orange and orange-yellow, for example. All other hues derive from more complex combinations and proportions of these elements.

The second quality of a color is its relative lightness or darkness, which is often called its value. Lightened, whitened hues are said to be tints, and dark hues that are tempered with black are called shades. The normal eye can differentiate among 100 values of a single color. The third quality of color is variously termed intensity, saturation or chroma, and refers to a color's purity or richness: the redness of red, the blueness of blue and so on.

Colors are said to be analogous, or related, if they are side by side on the color wheel — such as orange and orange-yellow. Complementary colors fall opposite each other on the wheel, as green and red do. Color schemes based on analogous colors are typically harmonious and restful, while schemes based on complementary colors can be exciting, kinetic, restless.

Colors are also characterized as warm or cool, depending upon the emotional impact they deliver. The warm colors are reds and yellows, the colors of sun and fire. Wherever they appear, they seem to advance, increasing the apparent size and vibrancy of the colored object or surface, so that they make surrounding spaces seem smaller. The cool colors — blues and greens — appear to recede from the viewer, diminishing the apparent size of objects and creating a sense of spaciousness and calm.

Whatever the intrinsic nature of a color may be, you modify it when you place it in a particular context. Consider the matter of lighting. Daylight is made up of all the colors of the spectrum, more or less evenly distributed; artificial lights are distinctly narrower and less balanced in their spectral ranges, with incandescent bulbs radiating more red than blue light waves and common fluorescents the reverse. Consequently, colors tend to look different in the store — under fluorescent light — than they do in the home, and different there depending upon the time of day.

Texture modifies color, too. Rough surfaces and matte finishes make colors appear darker, because irregular texture produces shadow and absorbs light. Additionally, colors interact when they neighbor each other: Light colors look lighter next to dark colors. And sometimes the eyes mix colors that are close together — in a small-patterned print, for example — to produce an unwanted blend.

With so many choices available, you can develop a pleasing assemblage of colors in many ways. The color wheel can be the starting point for schemes of varying complexity (pages 26-27), depending on how they are further refined and embellished with texture and pattern. Wallpapers, fabrics and rugs represent another source of color schemes; all you need do is repeat the colors of their different design elements — in appropriate proportions.

As you plan, you should collect paint manufacturers' color chips, and swatches of fabric, wallpaper and carpeting. Check the collection in daylight and at night; compare the scheme with that of adjoining rooms. Most important, consult your family. Everyone is entitled to opinions — which must be harmonized as the colors themselves are.

The wheel of paint pots at right shows the full spectrum of basic colors and the relationships between them. All other colors are produced by mixing these one with another, by adding black or white, and by increasing or diminishing the hue's intensity. Starting at top center and proceeding clockwise around the circle, the colors are red, red-orange, orange, orange-yellow, yellow, yellow-green, green, green-blue, blue, blue-purple, purple and purple-red.

Classic Combinations from the Color Wheel

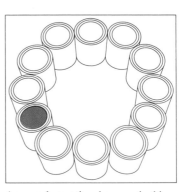

A monochromatic scheme — in this case, one exploring the family of blues in depth — must achieve variation and interest through different textures as well as different values of one hue. The result is a room that is serene in its color temperament, somewhat formal in feeling, and more spacious than its actual dimensions indicate. White accents — in the framed picture and shelves — provide relief notes. So, too, blue and white porcelain can be shown off to particular advantage on the shelves. Similar one-color schemes can be developed with virtually any hue, but to be successful you must do a delicate balancing act between too little contrast, which can be dull, and too much contrast, which can make the combination look busy. Check to see that the values harmonize both by day and by night, in the room for which they are intended, before committing yourself to a scheme: Subtlety is paramount here.

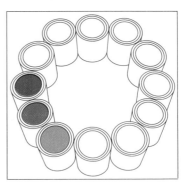

Analogous colors — which are any two or three neighbors on a wheel — provide the basis for a harmonious decorating partnership. Here, the blue of the couch and the armchair is played against its near relation green-blue in the walls, ceiling, carpet and throw pillows, and against blue-purple in draperies, painted shelving, cabinets and more pillows. Note that the green-blue and blue-purple analogues have versions of various values, all lighter than the basic blue: Hues of identical value tend to blend together. This scheme draws upon the cool side of the spectrum and is, consequently, particularly appropriate for a sunny, south-facing space or any room in a summer house. By the same token, warm, luminous analogues — orange-yellow to red-orange — can be a cheery mix in the cool light of a north-facing room or in a cold basement.

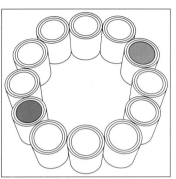

Complementary colors are any pair of hues that lie directly opposite each other on the color wheel: In this case, a primary color, blue, is complemented by a secondary, orange. Not only is the effect of a scheme built on such a pair sure to be lively, because there is maximum contrast between the hues, but both the warm and the cool zones of the spectrum are automatically represented. When working on a complementary color scheme, the wisdom is to make one of the pair the dominant player and use the other as contrast. In the scheme at left, for example, the intensity of the blue immediately establishes it as the dominant color, even though more of the surface area is covered in tints of orange. The choice of a predominantly blue painting on the wall is also an important factor here. Positioned over the blue sofa, it helps balance the blue of the draperies on the adjacent wall.

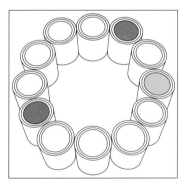

Split complementary is the term designers use for a scheme in which a hue is balanced against the two hues on either side of its complement. The effect is to tone down the contrast between complementary pairs but maintain the color punch. In this example, orange, which is the complement to blue and opposite it on the wheel, is replaced by its neighbors red-orange and orange-yellow. Because the neighboring colors have a tendency to mute each other's impact, they can be distributed more widely in a greater range of values. In the scheme at left, pale tints give a sense of height to the ceiling and make the walls seem to recede, especially in contrast to the dark shade of the carpet. Similar split-complementary schemes can be structured around combinations of red with green-blue and yellow-green, and purple with orange-yellow and yellow-green: Of all the basic approaches to color selection, this kind of scheme is the most versatile.

Choosing the right paint

Picking the right paint from the rows of cans lining a paint dealer's shelves — and figuring how much you need to buy — can be a daunting prospect. Fortunately, the paints used for interior walls belong to only a handful of types, which — despite the differences among manufacturers' formulations — share distinct characteristics, as this chart shows. (Stains, varnishes and other transparent wood finishes are discussed on pages 84-85.)

Most interiors are painted with either water-based latex paints or solvent-based alkyd paints. Both have modified forms to do special jobs: Textured paints, for a sculpted surface, and fire-retardant paints, which contain foaming agents that puff up when exposed to flames, are available in both latex and alkyd. Extrahard epoxies constitute a third category; they generally are used in areas subjected to extraordinary wear or on surfaces to which latex and alkyd will not adhere.

Every paint consists of two basic parts: a pigment and a vehicle. Pigments are finely ground minerals or chemicals that give paint color, density and opacity. Vehicles combine volatile liquid thinners ("volatile" because they evaporate as paint dries) and nonvolatile resins, the substances that harden into a tough film. The vehicle may also contain chemicals that speed drying time, increase film elasticity and prevent pigments from settling.

There are two kinds of thinner: water and organic solvents. The popular water-thinned latex interior paints contain emulsion polymer resins — usually acrylic or polyvinyl acetate. The resins are suspended in the water in microscopic droplets, forming an emulsion. When the water evaporates, the dispersed polymer resin particles — along with the pigments — coalesce to form the paint film.

Alkyd paints are thinned with organic solvents, such as mineral spirits. Their synthetic resins, modified with vegetable oils, are dissolved in solvent. As the volatile solvent evaporates, the resins oxidize: They unite chemically with oxygen in the air. The pigments and oxidized resins harden to a tough film. Oil-modified alkyd paints have almost totally replaced paints based on vegetable oils alone; the terms alkyd and oil-based often are used interchangeably.

The key differences between latex and alkyd paints stem from their vehicles. For example, latex paint is generally a poor choice for raw wood because the water swells wood fibers. But it makes a superb coating for fresh plaster because its thinner — water — is compatible with residual moisture in the plaster, and its oil-free resins are unaffected by masonry's alkalis. On the other hand, alkyd paint forms a tight, smooth finish on wood, but can blister and peel from fresh plaster because it seals in moisture and its oil-modified resins react chemically with the masonry.

Both latex and alkyd paints produce finishes in a broad gloss range, from flat, dull surfaces to hard, shiny ones. These differences are largely determined by the kinds and amounts of pigment in the paint. Most paint contains two types of pigment: prime and extender. Prime pigments give opacity and color. Extender pigments add strength and flexibility and play a major role in determining gloss.

The flat paint suitable for most walls and ceilings generally contains a lot of pigment, much of it extender pigment, such as calcium carbonate and silicates. High-gloss paint — used for woodwork and other areas subject to hard wear — generally contains less pigment and a high proportion of resin. By varying these ra-

A Paint for Every Surface

Paint	Characteristics	Raw Wood
Latex	Based on emulsion polymers, most commonly acrylic and polyvinyl acetate. Emulsified with water. Available in wide range of colors and finishes.	Not recommended for use directly on raw wood, plywood or particleboard: Water in paint may cause wood fibers to swell and adhesion may be poor. Prime wood first with alkyd primer or specially formulated latex primer recommended for wood.
Alkyd	Contains synthetic alkyd resins modified with vegetable oils, such as soya, linseed or castor oil; volatile organic solvents, such as mineral spirits. Dries by evaporation of solvent, plus oxidation of vegetable oils, leaving hard, elastic finish. Available in wide range of colors and finishes.	Suitable for direct use on all raw wood surfaces; use alkyd primer or sealer for best results.
Epoxy	Solvent-based paint containing epoxy resins. Dries to smooth, hard, impervious film. Ready-mixed form is similar in composition to alkyd paint. With two-package form, two components are combined in equal proportions before using; a chemical reaction takes place resulting in a mixture that produces a harder and more durable finish than ready-mixed type does. Available in limited range of colors; glossy and semigloss finishes only.	Ready-mixed paint and primer suitable on all raw woods.

tios, manufacturers create semigloss paints that dry to a smooth, hard surface with a soft sheen, suitable for kitchens, bathrooms and the like.

Unfortunately, the terms used on paint-can labels for these gloss levels have no precise, industry-wide meaning. One manufacturer's "low-luster" may be very unlike another's "eggshell," or "satin." And the term "enamel" — correctly employed for paint in which the pigments have been ground exceptionally fine — is sometimes associated with any extremely shiny surface, or is applied to semigloss alkyd paints. To tell for sure,

first consult a reputable dealer — and then see a sample of the paint after it dries.

For sampling, buy the smallest possible container of paint. For coating ceilings and walls, plan to use 1 gallon of paint to cover 350 square feet. To calculate amounts, multiply the length of the ceiling — in feet — by its width. For walls, multiply the height of each wall by its width, then total the figures; subtract the area of windows and doors only if they occupy almost an entire wall. Divide both results by 350 to determine the number of gallons. As a rule, the amount of trim — windows, doors, base and ceiling mold-

ing — is proportionate to the amount of wall space in roughly a 1 to 4 ratio. Accordingly, plan to buy 1 quart of trim paint for every gallon of wall paint.

When repainting, a single coat of paint generally will be all that is needed. However, a switch from a dark color to a lighter one almost always requires two coats. On surfaces that have never been painted — or on ones that have been previously coated with a finish that is incompatible with the new paint — an undercoat or primer provides a transition between the materials. The chart notes the appropriate primers for different circumstances.

New Plaster and Wallboard	New Masonry	Paint and Wallpaper	Advantages	Disadvantages
Suitable for direct use; however, applying latex primer-sealer first guarantees uniform finish coat.	Suitable for direct use; special latex masonry paint gives best results. Not affected by alkalis in concrete; porous paint film allows moisture below to evaporate, so paint does not blister or peel. Use latex primer if wall is mildewed, stained or patched; kill and remove any mildew before painting.	Adheres well to flat latex or alkyd paint. May not adhere well to hard glossy surfaces; sand old glossy finish before painting, then prime with alkyd or latex primer-sealer. Coat casein and calcimine water-based paints — found in some older houses — with calci-coater primer before applying latex. Not suitable for use over wallpaper; water in paint may soak paper, freeing it from wall.	Easy cleanup with soap and water. Retains color and gloss. Can be applied to damp surfaces. Dries in little more than an hour; two coats can be applied in a day. Easily recoated with other paints. Almost odorless. Spreads easily. Touch-up is simple; fresh paint blends in readily with old. Generally less expensive than alkyd paint of similar quality.	Only moderately resistant to stains and abrasion. High-gloss types not as glossy as alkyds. May absorb water, soften and peel if subjected to constant moisture.
Unsuitable for direct use on fresh plaster; allow plaster to dry for at least four weeks, then prime with latex primer. Raises nap on wallboard; prime first with latex primer.	Generally not suitable. Moisture trapped below paint may cause peeling; alkalis in masonry may affect oils in paint and cause blistering, peeling and loss of adhesion. Some alkyd paints are specially formulated for masonry; check labels for recommendations.	Suitable for direct use over wallpaper and latex or alkyd paint. May not adhere to glossy surfaces; sand glossy finishes or treat with a liquid deglosser. Use alkyd primer over surfaces in poor condition. Prime old casein and calcimine water-based paints with calci-coater primer. Sand old epoxy or urethane-coated surfaces.	Provides good coverage; often only one coat needed. Produces tight, elastic paint film that resists water and hard scrubbing; excellent for bathrooms and kitchens. Dries to hard, durable film. Good brushability; does not show lap marks. High stain resistance.	Cannot be applied to moist surfaces. Strong odor. Drying time up to 24 hours. Paint, and solvents used for thinning and cleanup, are toxic and flammable. Avoid contact with skin and clothing. Keep paint away from fire; provide ample ventilation; dispose of cleanup rags promptly in a metal container with a lid, or immerse them in water.
Not intended for use on plaster or wallboard.	Suitable for use directly on concrete, bricks, block and ceramic tile.	Works best on unpainted surfaces or over old epoxy finish. Strong volatile solvents may soften and wrinkle other paints.	Excellent resistance to abrasion, acids and alkalis. Two-package form adheres to otherwise unpaintable surfaces, such as porcelain and glass. Epoxy primers have excellent adhesion and provide a good base for latex or alkyd paints.	Expensive. May lose gloss and discolor if exposed to constant sunlight. Two-package form should be used within eight hours after mixing. Paint film takes about a week to reach maximum hardness. Special solvents used for thinning and cleanup are highly volatile and require extreme caution: Follow manufacturer's directions carefully; provide ample ventilation; wear goggles when pouring.

A guide to tools and techniques

Fresh paint is always a sure and inexpensive way to breathe new life into a room. And putting it on requires no special knack. The key to obtaining picture-perfect results is to approach the job systematically, following the numbered sequence shown below.

When painting a ceiling or a wall, first outline it with a brush (the technique, called "cutting in," is described in detail on pages 32-33), then fill in the large areas with a roller. Complete each area before moving on to the next; finish whatever ceiling or wall you are painting if you must stop for the day.

Correct tools are critical. You need a 2½-inch-wide trim brush for cutting in, and a 9-inch roller for large areas. In small or inaccessible areas, use a 3-inch trim roller; in these places a brush creates a texture noticeably different from that produced by a roller. However, in areas less than 3 inches wide, bristle marks are less conspicuous; use the trim brush there. For window frames and molding, use a 2-inch angled trim brush and a 1-inch sash brush.

Buy the best tools you can afford. The hallmark of a good brush is thick, flexible bristles that vary in length and appear frayed at the tips. These irregularities hold extra paint and apply it smoothly.

On a roller, the rotating sleeve should be wrapped in a spiral around a rigid plastic core; its edges should be beveled so as not to create ridges of wet paint on the wall. Use a metal spring-case roller frame that will hold the core firmly; add a 4-foot extension to reach the ceiling and the tops of walls. If you need a longer handle, buy a telescoping metal one; these commonly extend to 16 feet. Avoid handles made up of screw-in sections; they tend to wobble.

Match the tools to the paint. Water-based latex paint calls for a brush with synthetic bristles and a roller with a synthetic nap. Natural bristles and fibers absorb water from latex paint and lose their resiliency; choose them for applying alkyd paint. With rollers, use a $7/16$-inch to $1/2$-inch nap for flat paint, $1/4$- to $3/8$-inch for semigloss and high-gloss finishes.

Because there are subtle color differences between individual batches of the same paint, professional painters usually combine all of the paint for one coat in a single container. Mix paint in a 2- to 5-gallon bucket with a tight-fitting lid. Pour smaller amounts into an auxiliary pail or into the roller pan as you use the paint.

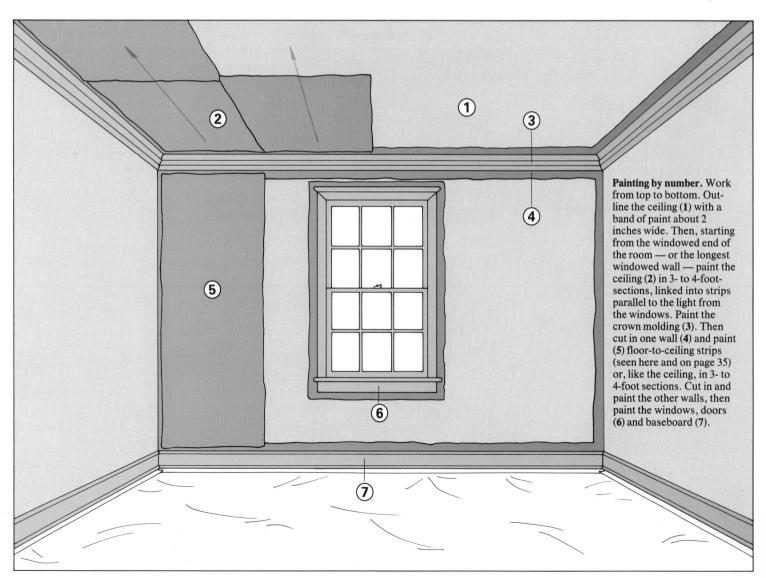

Painting by number. Work from top to bottom. Outline the ceiling (**1**) with a band of paint about 2 inches wide. Then, starting from the windowed end of the room — or the longest windowed wall — paint the ceiling (**2**) in 3- to 4-foot sections, linked into strips parallel to the light from the windows. Paint the crown molding (**3**). Then cut in one wall (**4**) and paint (**5**) floor-to-ceiling strips (seen here and on page 35) or, like the ceiling, in 3- to 4-foot sections. Cut in and paint the other walls, then paint the windows, doors (**6**) and baseboard (**7**).

Loading a paintbrush. Pour a layer of paint several inches deep into a pail; cover the paint can and set it aside. Dip the brush — in this case, a 2½-inch-wide trim brush — partway into the paint so that only the bottom third of the bristles is covered *(left)*. Tap one flat side of the bristles gently against the dry inner surface of the pail to remove excess paint; turn the brush and tap the other side of the bristles.

Loading a roller. Line a roller pan with a plastic roller-pan insert or aluminum foil. Fill the well of the pan half full with paint; set the paint can aside. Fit a wire roller grid over the sloping ramp of the pan. If you are using an extension handle, screw it into the threaded base of the roller's handle. Dip the roller into the well of the pan *(right)*, then roll it up and down the grid two or three times. Dip the roller again, and roll it back and forth over the grid until the sleeve is evenly saturated but does not drip.

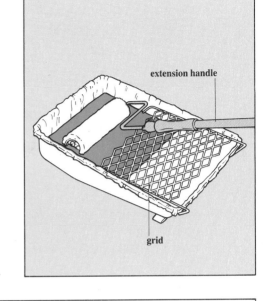

extension handle

grid

Mixing Your Own Colors

Like recipes of a cook's own devising, custom-mixed paint colors allow a decorator new freedom of expression. However, concocting colors is an art that takes practice to master. If you want to mix your own colors, start with pastel primaries; leave deep shades or blended hues until you have experience.

For the coloring agent, use the high-strength pigment called universal colorant, sold in tubes and squeeze bottles at paint and artist's-supply stores. For the base, choose pure white conventional wall paint; the colorant is equally compatible with latexes and alkyds.

The proportions can be varied to suit your taste, but the standard ratio is 1 ounce, or 2 measuring tablespoons, of colorant to 1 quart of paint. Because it is thicker, the colorant is difficult to mix into the base. To avoid streaks, dilute the colorant with a little base paint *(Step 1)*, then stir as much of this thinned colorant as desired into the remaining base. Next, refine the combination with the paint-mixing attachment of a power drill. (Both the drill and the attachment are inexpensive to buy, and they may also be rented.) Finally, to make sure that the mixed paint is absolutely smooth, filter it through cheesecloth.

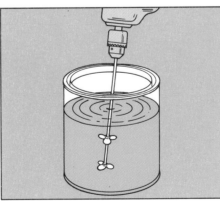

1 Diluting colorant. Pour some base paint into a disposable clear-plastic container. Add colorant — 2 tablespoons for each quart of paint being tinted. Using a wood paddle with ¼-inch-diameter holes drilled through its end to provide better paint flow, stir the colorant thoroughly into the base. Stirring constantly, pour the colored base little by little into the main supply of paint. When the paint appears to be the shade you want, paint a sample swatch in an inconspicuous place and allow it to dry. If necessary, add more of the colored base.

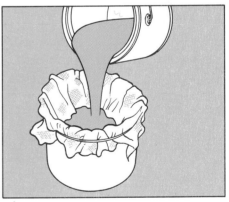

2 Power-mixing the tinted paint. Fit a variable-speed drill with a double-bladed metal paint-mixing attachment. With the drill turned off, immerse the mixer in the tinted paint and lower it until it touches the bottom of the container. Raise the drill an inch and turn on at low speed. Thoroughly mix the paint to blend in any traces of undissolved colorant. Then check the results by painting and drying a final test sample.

3 Filtering out impurities. Drape a layer of cheesecloth over a separate pail and secure the cloth to the rim with string or an elastic band. Pour the freshly mixed paint through this filter. Discard the filter and its collected deposits before using the paint.

Painting a Ceiling

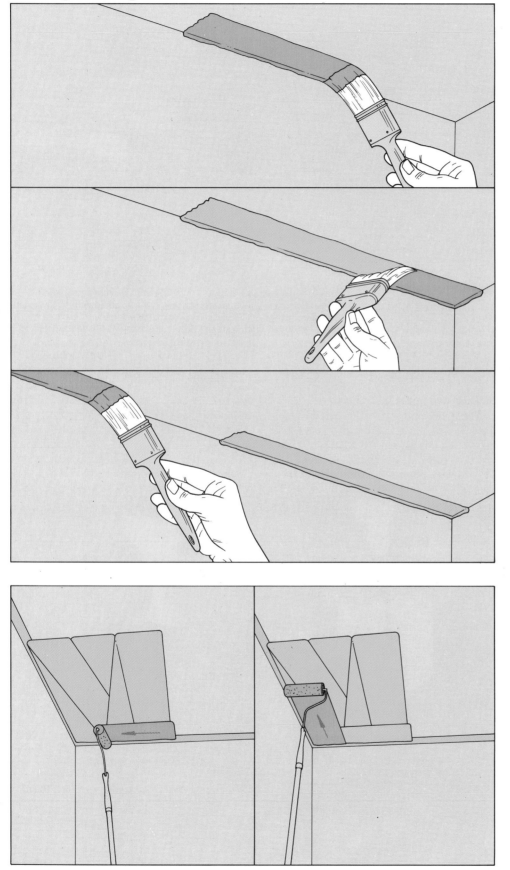

1 **Cutting in at the ceiling.** Starting two brush lengths from a corner, paint along the edge of the ceiling toward the corner *(left, top)* with a trim brush. Use long, overlapping strokes and keep the brush parallel to the edge. Allow a small amount of paint to flow onto the wall; you will create an even line when you paint the wall *(opposite, below)*. When you reach the corner, reverse the angle of the brush and lightly draw it back along the strip you just painted *(center)* to smooth out the brushstrokes. Repeat these strokes around the entire perimeter of the ceiling, always starting the initial brushstroke on a dry section and painting into a wet section *(bottom)*.

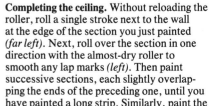

4 **Completing the ceiling.** Without reloading the roller, roll a single stroke next to the wall at the edge of the section you just painted *(far left)*. Next, roll over the section in one direction with the almost-dry roller to smooth any lap marks *(left)*. Then paint successive sections, each slightly overlapping the ends of the preceding one, until you have painted a long strip. Similarly, paint the rest of the ceiling, section by section, in parallel strips beginning at the windowed wall.

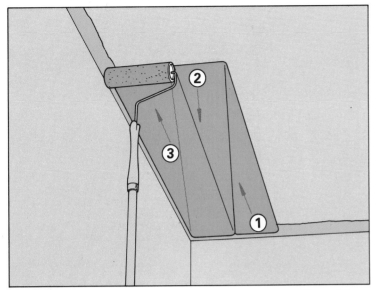

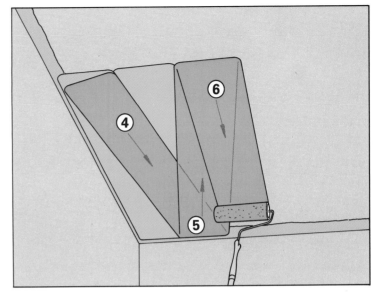

2 **Painting a ceiling section.** Fit an extension into the threaded base of the roller handle. Stand about 4½ feet from the windowed wall, facing toward it. Place a paint-filled roller one roller width from a corner of the ceiling. Without changing your stance, pull the roller toward yourself and away from the wall (**1**) as far as you comfortably can — about 4 feet. Without removing the roller from the ceiling, push it back into the corner (**2**) and out again (**3**) closely parallel to the wall. Use light, even pressure for each stroke and work slowly to avoid spinning paint into the air.

3 **Continuing the section.** With the roller still on the ceiling, roll back across the first strips you made (**4**), and with two additional strokes (**5** and **6**) apply one more roller width to the unpainted surface. The result will be a painted section about 4 feet long and a little less than 3 feet wide.

Painting a Wall

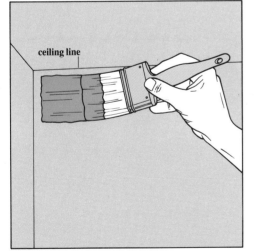

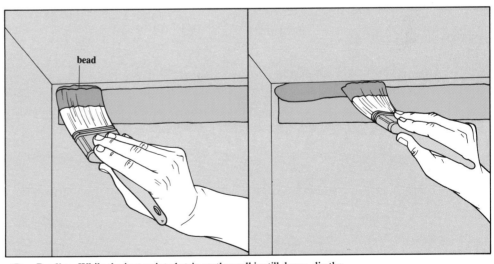

1 **Cutting in on a wall.** Start on the wall with the most interruptions such as electric fixtures, windows and doors. Working from the upper left corner if you are right-handed, or from the upper right corner if left-handed, use a fully loaded trim brush to make a long backhand stroke below the ceiling line or molding. Leave a ¼-inch space at the edge of the ceiling or molding, and paint the strip only as long as you can reach comfortably without moving the ladder.

2 **Beading.** While the just-painted strip on the wall is still damp, dip the brush back into the paint. Grasp the brush as shown above, left, and gently press the bristle tips flat about ¹⁄₁₆ inch from the top of the wall. A thin line of paint — the bead — will rise to the tips. Without taking the bristles from the wall, slowly raise the brush to a 45° angle *(right)*. Then, in one smooth, steady motion, gently drag the brush along the top of the wall as far as you can comfortably reach. Allow a minute line of paint to run up onto the ceiling; this will create the effect of a perfect seam. ▶

3 **Laying off the cut-in strip.** To smooth out the ridges of paint that accumulate during beading, and to feather the lower edge of the cut-in strip, wipe the brush on the rim of the paint pail, then draw it along the cut-in strip with a backhand motion like that pictured in Step 1 on the preceding page. When you reach the end of the strip, reverse the angle of the brush and draw it lightly back along the paint line *(right)*. Professionals call this process — the last stage of cutting in — "laying off" the paint.

Move the ladder and repeat Steps 1 through 3 to cut in the rest of the ceiling line. Then cut in down the sides of the wall, along the baseboard and around the windows and any doors. On those areas where a precise line of demarcation is unnecessary — at the junction of two walls to be painted the same color, for example — omit Step 2.

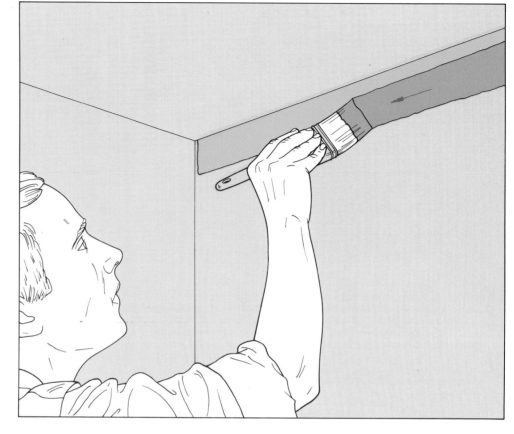

5 **Painting a small wall area.** To paint a narrow or hard-to-reach section of the wall — the area between baseboard and window, for example — first remove the roller's extension handle. Then load the roller and roll paint onto the wall either vertically or horizontally, whichever is less tiring.

For areas that are especially inaccessible, use a trim roller, or in an area less than 3 inches wide, a trim brush.

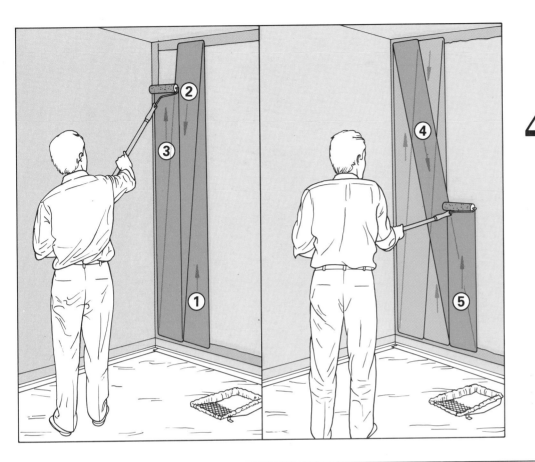

4 **Rolling the paint.** Starting at a bottom corner of the outlined wall, position the filled roller about one roller width from the vertical cut-in line. Keeping a light, steady pressure on the handle, push the roller up to the cut-in line at the ceiling with a single slow stroke *(far left, 1)*, then draw the roller back down into the corner (**2**). Apply a third swath (**3**) parallel to the end of the wall and as close to the adjacent wall as possible.

Roll diagonally back across the strips you just painted *(left, 4)*, and then up to the ceiling (**5**) to apply one more roller width of paint to the wall. With each successive stroke, gradually increase the pressure on the roller. The five strokes will produce a painted section three roller widths wide, from floor to ceiling. Paint a second five-stroke strip next to and slightly overlapping the first section. Continue until you have completed the entire wall.

Painting Molding

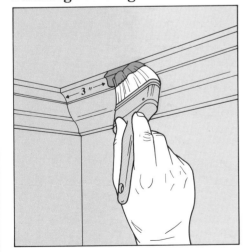

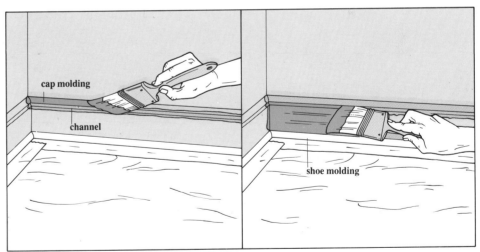

Painting ceiling molding. Rest the bristles of a 2½-inch trim brush just below the top of the molding — here, crown molding — about 3 inches from a corner. Exert light pressure on the bristle tips so a bead of paint rises to the top of the molding, then draw the bead 2 feet along the molding *(above)*. Reverse the angle of the brush and paint back into the corner. Pointing the bristles down, use the same technique to paint the bottom of the molding. Then paint the molding's face.

Painting a baseboard. With an angled trim brush, paint one 3-foot section of the channel below the cap molding. Dip the brush into the paint, tap it against the side of the pail, then wipe it across the rim. Holding the brush as shown above, left, rest the bristles just below the molding's top. Put light pressure on the tips to raise a bead, and gently draw the brush along the molding for 3 feet. Finish the channel and cap molding on that wall.

Then paint the bottom of the baseboard, pointing the bristles down to lay the bead just above the shoe molding. (Shoe molding is customarily finished like the floor. If you want to paint yours, lay the bead just above the floor line.) Finally, hold the brush parallel to the floor *(above, right)*, and paint the face of the baseboard.

Painting a Window

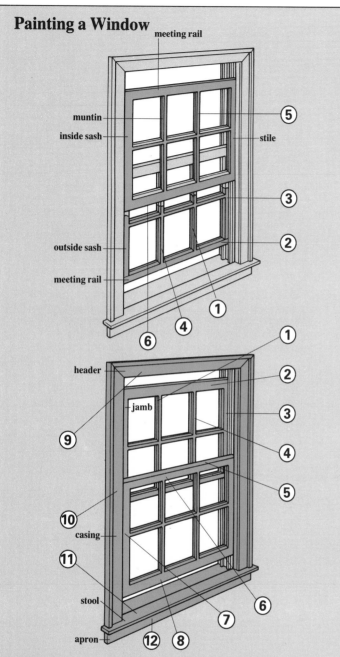

meeting rail

muntin

inside sash

stile

5

3

2

outside sash

meeting rail

1

4

6

header

1

2

jamb

3

9

4

10

5

casing

11

stool

6

7

apron

12 8

Painting a Door

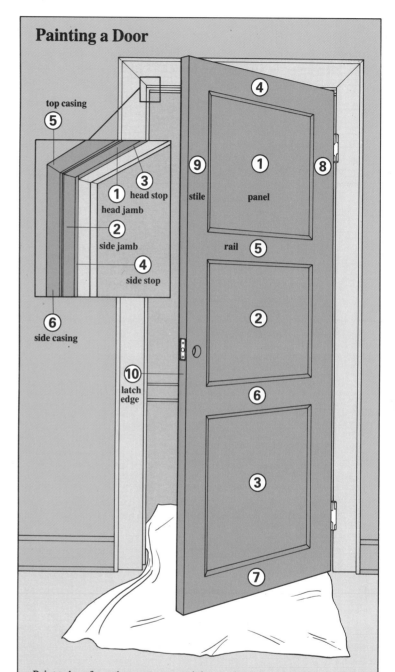

top casing

5

4

3

9

1

8

1 head stop

head jamb

2

side jamb

stile

panel

4

side stop

rail

5

6

2

side casing

6

10

latch
edge

3

7

Paint a window in an orderly fashion, using the numbered sequence above to reach parts obstructed by the inner sash — and to avoid overlooking other sections. First, raise the inside sash, lower the outside one and paint the inside surfaces of the muntins, or pane dividers, surrounding each lower pane in the outside sash *(top, 1)*. Next, paint the front face of the outside sash's meeting rail (2) and the exposed lower portions of its stiles (3). Paint the muntin faces (4). Then move up to the inside sash and paint its muntins (5). Finally, paint the inside sash's bottom edge (6).

Pressing against unpainted surfaces, lower the inside sash and raise the outside, reversing their positions *(above)*. On the outside sash, paint the insides of the muntins (2), the top rail's front (2), the unpainted portions of the stiles (3) and the muntin faces (4). To finish the inside sash, paint the meeting rail's top (5), the meeting rail's face (6), the stiles (7) and the bottom rail (8). Let the paint dry, then paint the underside of the header above the sashes (9) and the window casing (10). Allow those surfaces to dry. Finally, paint the top and lip of the stool (11) and the apron (12).

Paint a door from the center out and the top down, starting with the panel moldings, then filling in the panels themselves (1-3). Next, paint the rails (4-7) and stiles (8-9). If the door swings into the room you are painting, as in this example, paint the latch edge of the door (10); if it swings out, paint the hinge edge of the door. Then paint the head jamb *(inset, 1)*, the side jamb (2), and the head and side stops (3, 4). On an inward-swinging door, such as the one above, paint only those narrow edges of the stops that face you; if the door swings out of the room, paint both the front and side edges of the stops — the parts that remain visible after the door is closed. Finally, paint the doorframe. Start with the upper edge of the top casing, followed by its face (5). Finally, paint the edges of the side casings and their faces (6).

Scaffolding for a Stairwell

If you are painting the upper walls and the ceiling above a stairwell, you will need to stand on a platform. You can construct a sturdy one with a straight ladder, a stepladder and a 2-by-10 scaffold-grade plank — an extra-strong piece of lumber available from a lumber dealer. (If the plank must span more than 6 feet, buy two of them and set one on top of the other for added strength.)

To assemble the platform, place the straight ladder on the stairs, resting its upper ends against the wall. Protect the surface of the wall by wrapping the ladder's upper ends with rags.

Set the stepladder at the head of the stairs and lay the plank across its lowest rung and whichever rung of the straight ladder makes the plank level.

A Power Roller to Save Time

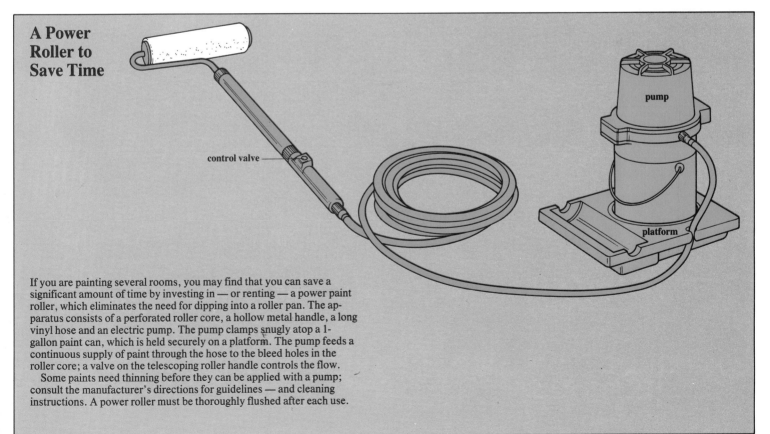

control valve

pump

platform

If you are painting several rooms, you may find that you can save a significant amount of time by investing in — or renting — a power paint roller, which eliminates the need for dipping into a roller pan. The apparatus consists of a perforated roller core, a hollow metal handle, a long vinyl hose and an electric pump. The pump clamps snugly atop a 1-gallon paint can, which is held securely on a platform. The pump feeds a continuous supply of paint through the hose to the bleed holes in the roller core; a valve on the telescoping roller handle controls the flow.

Some paints need thinning before they can be applied with a pump; consult the manufacturer's directions for guidelines — and cleaning instructions. A power roller must be thoroughly flushed after each use.

Textures to enrich a wall

Textured wall surfaces can capture the ever-intriguing play of light and shadow, an effect achieved simply by applying and shaping a grainy, plaster-like material called texturing compound. The texture created depends mainly on the finishing tool used. The stucco-like peaks directly below are made with a roller *(page 40, top)*, the feathery swirls below, right, with a stiff-bristled brush *(pages 40-41, bottom)*, and the curved ridges at bottom left with a trowel *(page 41, top)*.

Texturing compound comes only in off-white, gray, and sand tones, but you can change the color of your wall as little as a day after texturing it. Use latex paint and a roller with a thick (¾-inch) nap.

The compound covers many defects, but some walls may need preparation.

Loose or scaling paint must be scraped off. A day in advance, spackle any holes deeper than ¼ inch. Over new wallboard, apply vinyl primer-sealer. Sand glossy paint with coarse sandpaper to give it tooth; flat paint needs no special care.

For applying and smoothing the compound, you will need only two tools: a taping knife with a blade 10 inches wide, and a broad knife *(Step 1, opposite)* 6 inches wide. Then choose your finishing tool according to the texture desired.

The compound is applied in 3-foot-wide strips from ceiling to floor. Once you have covered a strip of wall, smooth the compound and texture it before covering the next strip. The compound stays workable for half an hour, or up to 45 minutes if sprayed lightly with water from a plant mister. Work fast enough that the edge of a finished strip will still blend with fresh compound applied to the next strip. You may wish to practice on a scrap board before you start work on the wall.

Before using the compound, mix it to an even consistency. On first opening the container, pour any liquid from atop the compound into a jar. Transfer half the compound to a second bucket, then pour half the liquid into each batch and mix both batches with the taping knife. Seal one batch and set it aside until needed.

Cover the floor with dropcloths and keep a damp rag handy for wiping stray compound from woodwork. If you must interrupt the job for more than 15 minutes, complete a wall first; wash your tools in water and cover the compound. At the end of the job, leftover compound will keep for a year if stored airtight.

Dressing the Wall with Compound

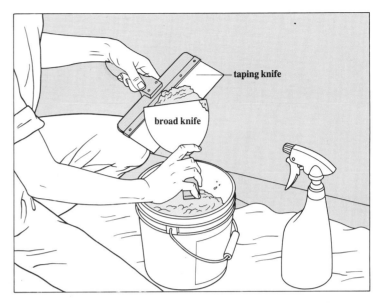

1 **Loading the taping knife and broad knife.** Pick up the 6-inch-wide broad knife in your dominant hand (the woman pictured here is right-handed), and hold the taping knife in your other hand, as shown. Use the broad knife to scoop ½ cup of compound out of the bucket and onto the front (palm side) of the broad knife. Turn the knife over and scrape the compound off onto the taping knife, as shown at right. Then turn the broad knife front (palm) side up again and use it to scrape about half the compound off the face of the taping knife. Use these two scraping movements to transfer the compound back and forth from broad knife to taping knife until you feel comfortable with the technique and can handle the compound with minimum spillage.

2 **Applying the compound.** With about a cup of compound on the blade of the taping knife, stand on a ladder and face the top left corner of the wall. Take ½ cup of compound onto the palm side of the broad knife and apply the compound with a smearing motion, keeping the face of the blade at about a 10° angle to the wall, as shown at right. Spread the compound to cover about a square foot, in a layer 1/16 inch to 1/8 inch thick; then reload the broad knife from the taping knife and repeat for the next square foot of the wall. When the taping knife is empty, use the broad knife to reload it from the bucket. Cover an area about 1 foot high and 3 feet wide; work the compound up to the ceiling and over to the wall. Then go on to the 3 square feet immediately below. Continue applying the compound until you have covered a strip 3 feet wide, from ceiling to floor. Spray the strip lightly with water from a spray bottle.

3 **Smoothing the surface.** Use the taping knife as shown at right to smooth the layer of compound. Keep the face of the blade at a 10° angle to the wall; do not add new compound to the wall, and apply just enough pressure to level out the surface. Sweep the knife lightly across the wet area in long, straight lines. If texturing compound builds up on the face of the taping knife, scrape it off with the broad knife and return it to the bucket. After smoothing one 3-foot-wide strip, give it the desired finished texture *(pages 40-41)* before applying more compound.

A Stucco Effect from a Roller

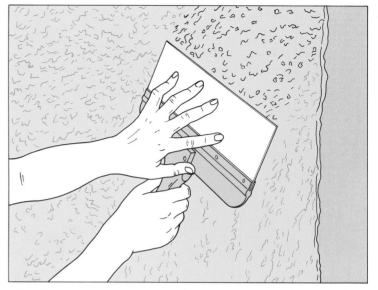

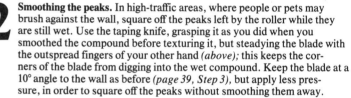

1 **Making stucco-like peaks.** Use a plastic texturing roller, or a short-napped synthetic-fiber roller that you have moistened with water. Move the roller back and forth in 2-foot strokes, slowly enough that the roller rotates and does not skid. Apply light pressure, maintaining contact with the compound but not pushing into it. Move the roller in an irregular, overlapping pattern (above); at the end of each stroke, do not lift the roller, but angle it slightly so that when you reverse direction, it covers a new section of the wall. At the top and bottom of a strip, run the roller horizontally to texture the edges. Finish texturing a 3-foot-wide ceiling-to-floor strip before you apply compound to the adjacent strip.

2 **Smoothing the peaks.** In high-traffic areas, where people or pets may brush against the wall, square off the peaks left by the roller while they are still wet. Use the taping knife, grasping it as you did when you smoothed the compound before texturing it, but steadying the blade with the outspread fingers of your other hand (above); this keeps the corners of the blade from digging into the wet compound. Keep the blade at a 10° angle to the wall as before (page 39, Step 3), but apply less pressure, in order to square off the peaks without smoothing them away.

Feathery Swirls from a Brush

Making half-moons. With your fingers above the handle and your thumb below, hold a stiff-bristled texturing brush horizontally, perpendicular to the wall. Press the tips of the bristles into the compound and move the brush in a semicircular arc 9 or 10 inches across. As you move the brush through the arc, turn your hand over, so that you finish the stroke with your thumb uppermost. While the brush is still in motion, lift it away from the wall. Repeat the stroke, beginning 5 inches from the start of the first stroke and crossing its end.

Curved Ridges from a Trowel

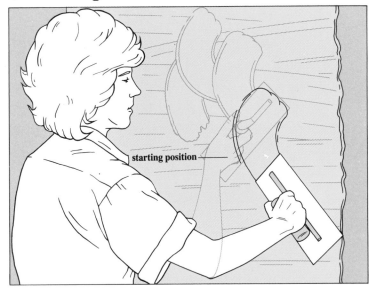

1 **Making a trowel stroke.** Beginning near the wall's top left corner, hold the trowel with its long edges 45° from the vertical, as seen in the starting position above. Press it lightly against the wall at a slight angle, so that the top 4 inches of the tool touch the wet compound and the bottom end of the trowel does not. Move the trowel counterclockwise in a small (1-foot radius) quarter circle, simultaneously rotating the trowel counterclockwise by turning your wrist as you move your arm. The top edge of the tool will leave a smooth, flat surface, and the top outside corner will leave a curved ridge. Lift the trowel away from the wall while still moving it in the direction of the stroke. Start the next stroke 5 inches to the right, so that it swoops across the beginning of the first stroke.

2 **Varying the strokes.** To minimize trowel prints on the wall, the trowel should be in motion as you bring it into contact with the wall at the beginning of each stroke, as well as when you lift it away from the wall at the end of a stroke. Reverse the movement shown in Step 1, to make clockwise texturing strokes with the trowel. Align each stroke so that it covers the beginning or end of a previous stroke. Continue across and down the wall, mixing clockwise and counterclockwise strokes for an interesting, irregular pattern.

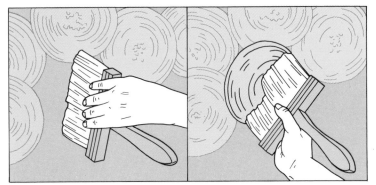

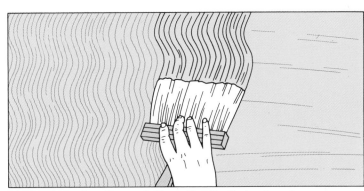

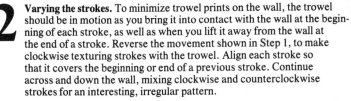

Making circles. Grasp the brush between your fingers and thumb, keeping your thumb at the base of the handle. Start with the brush in the position shown above, left, and rotate it by pivoting it around your thumb, keeping the brush perpendicular to the wall (*above, right*). To avoid leaving a brushprint across the circle, lift the brush away from the wall while still moving it. Then reposition it on the wall so that the bristles at one end of the brush slightly overlap your last circle, and turn the brush again. Repeat all across and down the wall.

Making ripples. Standing on a ladder and holding the brush as shown above, place the tips of the bristles at a 45° angle against the top of the wall. Draw the brush steadily down the wall while moving your hand from side to side in a regular rhythm; the sidewise distance should be between 1 and 2 inches. Continue the pattern as far down as you can comfortably reach without climbing down the ladder, then return to the top and make another ripple stroke beside the first. When you reach the edge of the compound-covered section, get down off the ladder to start the lower half of the strip. Blend the strokes below with the ones above by having your brush in motion before it touches the wall. Finally, finish the section with ripple strokes that run upward for a foot or so from the wall's bottom edge, lifting the brush from the wall while still moving it in the side-to-side pattern.

Artistry with custom glazes

Translucent colored glazes, applied with patterned effects, add depth and richness to painted surfaces, giving walls their own vibrant visual personalities. By experimenting with the six application techniques shown on the following pages, you can achieve infinitely variable effects, ranging from a formal plaid (below) to a subtle matte finish or bold black streaks on red (opposite).

A glaze's pattern can be created in two basic, quite different ways. A soft-edged finish that largely obscures the underlying paint is created by painting a wall with a thin film of glaze, then quickly removing much of the wet glaze with a dry paintbrush, a damp sponge or a rag wrapped in cheesecloth. A sharper-edged glaze that reveals more of the wall's original color is created by applying random bits of glaze with a dry sponge, a textured-paint roller or a twisted rag.

Because glazing is a somewhat messy enterprise, you will need a dropcloth for the floor and some other items: 3-inch drafting tape (available at art-supply shops) for masking the edges of the ceiling and trim molding, vinyl painter's gloves to protect your hands, a large pad of newsprint or a roll of butcher's paper, and many clean cotton rags.

Tips on choosing colors and instructions for mixing the glaze are given on page 44. To test the final color of your glaze, prime and paint a few scraps of wallboard, birch plywood or surfaced lumber to match your wall's color. Then mix the glaze and rehearse the technique on the scrap test panels several times.

Practice is particularly important for the soft-edged finishes: You must learn to work quickly, since the wet glaze will become too tacky to manipulate in a bare five minutes.

Should a section of glaze turn tacky before you finish it, you may be able to redeem the situation: Dip a dry 4-inch paintbrush in mineral spirits, wipe off the excess with a rag and judiciously brush the remaining spirits into the glaze. The same method can be used to soften or remove hardened glaze at the edges of a section. And if all else fails, you can wipe away the unsightly glaze with a spirits-soaked rag and redo the section.

When the glazing job is completed, let the coating cure for two days. Then cover it with a protective layer of semi-gloss alkyd varnish.

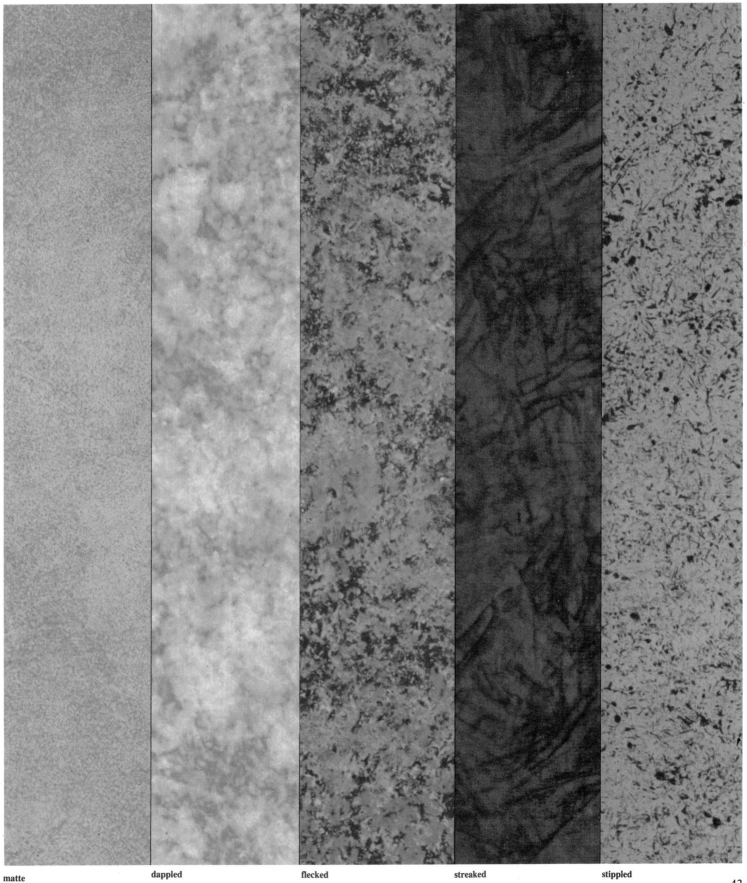

matte   dappled   flecked   streaked   stippled

A Layering of Colors

The character of a wall color can be dramatically altered by the application of a thin tinted glaze that allows some of the underlying paint to show through. Here, the horizontal strips of base color are green, white and blue, seen uncovered in the central vertical column. Those colors are infused with new liveliness by glazes — medium blue in the left vertical column and medium green in the right.

Semigloss paints make the most suitable base coat. Glazes tend to slide and mottle over glossy paint, and flat paint gives a dull finish to a glazed wall. Nonporous alkyd paint yields a sharp, bright impression when glazed; latex paint usually provides a softer, more muted effect.

The full spectrum of glaze colors can be used over white. A different shade of the wall color can give a subtle tone-on-tone effect (as in the blue-on-blue and green-on-green sections here); use a lighter shade of glaze for a dark wall and a darker glaze for a light wall. Or you can combine related or complementary colors.

Mixing the Glaze

The techniques described on these pages employ homemade glazes with four basic ingredients: japan paint (an intensely colored mixture of pigment and varnish) and canned glaze coat, both available from art-supply stores, and white semigloss alkyd enamel and mineral spirits, available from paint stores. Strikingly different effects can be created simply by changing the colors and proportions of these ingredients according to the recipe given with each technique.

To mix the glaze, you will need wooden mixing paddles, some cheesecloth, and one-quart and half-gallon glass jars with lids — old pickle or mayonnaise jars are fine. To estimate the amount of glaze needed, allow a half gallon of glaze for every 400 square feet of wall area.

1 **Straining the pigments.** In a one-quart glass jar, stir together the japan paint and the white enamel (if any is called for) with a wooden mixing paddle. Mark the mixture's level on a piece of masking tape on the jar, so you can measure out an equal amount of glaze coat later. Stretch a single thickness of cheesecloth across the mouth of a half-gallon jar and secure it with a rubber band. Slowly pour the viscous mixture onto the cheesecloth and press it into the jar with the rounded bowl of a spoon (above).

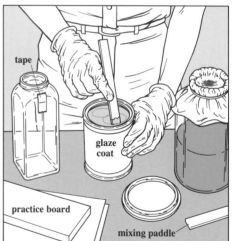

2 **Mixing the glaze.** With a clean paddle, thoroughly stir a can of glaze coat. Fill the quart jar with glaze coat to the level marked in Step 1. Remove the cheesecloth from the half-gallon jar and add the measured glaze coat to the mix in the jar. To adjust the glaze's color, add equal amounts of glaze coat and pigment, using more white enamel in the pigment portion of the mixture to get a lighter tone, less for a darker tone. Using a larger container, mix the mineral spirits, if any, into the glaze just before applying it.

A Fine-Textured Plaid Glaze

Like a fine hand-woven fabric, the plaid glaze at right imparts quiet distinction to its surroundings, particularly in a formal space such as a dining room. The plaid effect is created by dragging a dry paintbrush vertically through a coat of wet glaze, then two days later dragging the brush horizontally through a second wet coat. You may choose to use the brush only once, leaving simple vertical striations. By varying the pressure on the brush you can alter the color balance between the base coat and the glaze. Here, heavy pressure was applied to reveal streaks of white wall; lighter pressure would have allowed far less white to show through the two layers of blue glaze.

The basic recipe for all dragged glazes uses 1 quart of pigment (here Prussian blue japan paint, but for pastels a mixture of japan paint and white enamel), 1 quart of glaze coat and 1 quart of mineral spirits, mixed according to the instructions on the previous page. Once you start the job, concentrate on working not only rapidly, but neatly; smudges will be glaringly visible on the linear pattern.

1 **Dragging the brush vertically.** Cover the edges of ceiling molding and the baseboard with 3-inch drafting tape. Have a helper with a 4-inch brush apply a thin coat of glaze 18 inches wide from the ceiling to the baseboard at the wall's right end (assuming that you are right-handed). While the helper uses another ladder to apply additional vertical strips, place your stepladder about 1 foot from the wall. Grasp the bristles of a dry 4-inch brush at their base with both hands. Press the brush firmly against the tape above the wet glaze and drag the brush downward steadily, descending the ladder without interrupting the continuous brushstroke, until you reach the baseboard. If you hesitate at all during the stroke, return to the ceiling and redo the entire stroke. After the stroke, clean the brush by grasping and wiping its bristles repeatedly with a dry rag. Continue dragging the wall with barely overlapping strokes while your helper applies glaze in front of you. Proceed directly to Step 2. ▶

3-inch drafting tape

wet glaze

tape   baseboard

2 **Removing excess glaze.** When the wall is coated with fresh glaze 2 feet beyond where you are dragging the brush, tell your helper to put aside the glaze-laden brush temporarily. While you continue with your dragging strokes, have the helper dip a 2-inch brush in mineral spirits and brush off most of the spirits on a rag. Then, along the top and bottom of the dragged area, where excess glaze has accumulated, the helper should lightly brush sideways with the bristles, once in each direction, to remove the extra glaze. Continue with the vertical strokes along the entire wall while your helper alternately applies glaze in front of you and brushes the edges of the dragged glaze behind you. Let the glaze dry for two days.

3 **Adding horizontal lines.** Have your helper apply the second coat to the upper half of the wall in 4-foot-square sections, starting at the upper right and brushing horizontally. As each square is covered, drag the dry brush across the glaze *(above),* working your way down the square with overlapping strokes. Stagger the places where you end the strokes by a few inches. Have your helper remove excess glaze at the end of each stroke *(Step 2).* Then lap the start of strokes for the next section about 2 inches over the ends of the completed strokes. When applying glaze to the lower half of the wall, the helper should brush mineral spirits into the lower border of the already-dragged upper section to soften the glaze there. Then start dragging the lower section of the wall along that rewetted border.

A Cloudy Finish

The translucent matte finish at right has the look of fragile clouds. The subtlest and most versatile of all glazing effects, it also is one of the simplest to create. It is produced by painting glaze on with a brush, then repeatedly stamping the wall with a cheesecloth pad that removes tiny, irregular traces of the wet glaze.

The cloud glaze includes about 1 pint of japan paint (here, 1 pint of C.P. — for chromium pure — medium green, tinted with 4 extra teaspoons of cobalt blue), 1 pint of white semigloss alkyd enamel, 1 quart of glaze coat and 1 quart of mineral spirits. Here, the glaze was applied over white semigloss enamel.

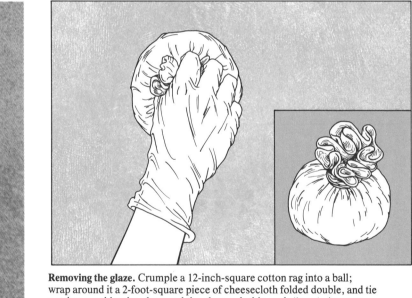

Removing the glaze. Crumple a 12-inch-square cotton rag into a ball; wrap around it a 2-foot-square piece of cheesecloth folded double, and tie a string or rubber band around the cheesecloth's neck *(inset).* As your helper paints the wall with glaze, grasp the cheesecloth pad at its neck and pat it firmly against the glazed wall. Taking care not to slide across the surface, pat each newly glazed section of wall until you obtain a cloudlike finish that reveals a hint of the wall's underlying color. Every few minutes, when the pad becomes saturated and no longer absorbs glaze, replace the cheesecloth and expose a clean portion of the wadded rag; occasionally replace the rag.

A Softly Dappled Glaze

The dappled effect at right is created by brushing on glaze and then removing most of it by lightly patting the wall with a sponge dampened with mineral spirits. The sponge lifts some glaze and the spirits soften the remaining imprint. By varying how much the sponge pats overlap, you can control the amount of glaze removed and thus the wall's color.

The sponging technique is simplicity itself if you observe two simple rules. Use a natural sponge to achieve a variable imprint; a synthetic sponge creates a hard-edged, repetitive pattern. And thoroughly wring mineral spirits from the sponge, lest excess spirits cause beads of diluted glaze to puddle or run down the wall. If this happens, wipe off the marred glaze with a spirits-soaked rag and start anew.

The glaze recipe for this sponging technique uses 8 ounces of japan paint (here, 4 ounces each of cobalt blue and turkey red colors), 24 ounces of white alkyd enamel, 1 quart of glaze coat and 8 ounces of mineral spirits. Here, it has been applied over white semigloss enamel.

Sponging the wall. Have your helper use a 4-inch brush to paint the top half of the wall from right to left with a thin coat of glaze. As the helper proceeds, dip a natural sponge about 4 inches in diameter in a bowl of mineral spirits and wring out the sponge until it is virtually dry. Following closely behind the helper, pat the glaze quickly and lightly with the sponge in an irregular, overlapping pattern. When the sponge becomes saturated with glaze and no longer removes color from the wall, rinse it in mineral spirits and wring it out again. Paint and sponge the bottom half of the wall in the same way.

A Crisply Flecked Glaze

The sharply defined edges of the finely flecked glaze at right are created simply by patting glaze onto a wall with a sponge. This technique can be used with one, two or three glaze colors, either colors that contrast markedly with the wall and with each other, as here, or related colors that blend with subtle gradations. Usually the lightest color is applied first, followed by progressively darker tones. In the example here, a Prussian blue wall was covered first with random flecks of beige glaze and then with a light blue glaze, until only small flecks of dark blue remained exposed.

The basic recipe for glazes applied by sponge uses about 1 pint of pigment (a mixture of white enamel and japan paint), 1 pint of glaze coat and 1 pint of mineral spirits. In this example, the first glaze was pigmented with 4 teaspoons of raw umber japan paint and 1 quart of white enamel, the second glaze by 8 ounces of permanent blue japan paint, 4 teaspoons of raw umber japan paint and 24 ounces of white enamel.

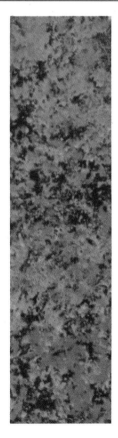

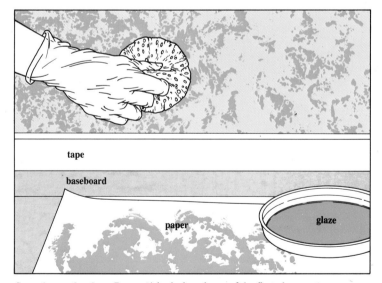

tape

baseboard

paper

glaze

Sponging on the glaze. Pour a ¼-inch-deep layer of the first glaze onto a plate and dip a dry natural sponge in the glaze. To remove excess glaze, pat the sponge on a sheet of paper about six times, until it leaves a neat pattern without smearing, dribbling, or leaving a thick, wet imprint. Then firmly pat the sponge on the wall in the same way, spacing the imprints to cover perhaps 60 per cent of the wall's surface and rotating the sponge frequently between imprints to avoid a repetitive pattern. Reload the sponge with glaze every 15 strokes or so, pat the excess glaze onto the paper and continue in the same way, covering the entire wall with randomly spaced imprints. Let the first coat of glaze set for one day. Apply a second (and, if you wish, a third) glaze color in the same way.

A Boldly Streaked Glaze

By far the most dramatic glaze effect is the streaked pattern at right, created by rolling a wrinkled cylinder of glaze-covered rags on the wall. This technique works well with strongly contrasting colors, here a black glaze on a dark red wall. Exercise judicious restraint in applying this method; overworking the pattern with too many streaks will produce a messy appearance.

Rag rolling also requires considerable preliminary practice on sheets of paper and on test boards. Use them to determine how many times to roll a section of the wall and how much paint to brush onto the roller *(Step 1 at top, opposite)*. If at first you overload the roller with paint, you can wring it out and reuse it. You also can experiment with first dipping the dry roller in mineral spirits, wringing it out, and then applying the paint to it; the effect will be to soften the pattern's edges.

The recipe for a high-contrast rolled glaze uses 1 quart of japan paint (here, lamp black), 1 quart of glaze coat and 1 quart of mineral spirits.

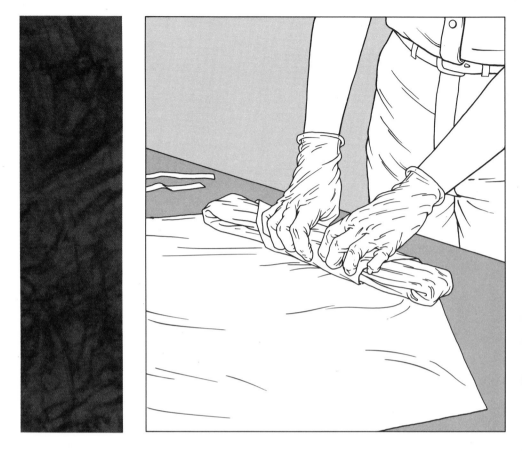

A Stippled Glaze

Unlike most glaze patterns, the stippled effect at right relies on an interplay of texture and shadow as well as on color. Here, the glaze color contrasts mildly with that of the wall's base coat — a green glaze on a gray wall — to blend easily into almost any room.

A stippled glaze is applied with unlikely tools: a paint roller and an edger (available separately or in a kit) that originally were designed to finish the surface of textured paint *(pages 38-41)*. These tools have a thick, matted nap of plastic loops that rapidly applies glaze in an irregular pattern of droplets and lines.

To prevent drips, a stippled glaze is thicker than other types and contains no thinning mineral spirits. The basic recipe uses 1 quart of pigment (here, C.P. — for chromium pure — green medium japan paint, but for pastels a blend of paint and white enamel) and 1 quart of glaze coat.

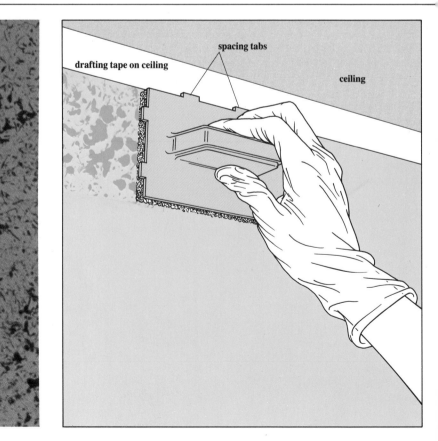

1 **Making the roller.** Lay a rag 18 inches square on a worktable. Grasp a matching-size rag at opposing corners and roll it into a loose cylinder, then fold its ends together. Starting at one corner of the flat rag, roll the cylindrical rag up in it *(left)*. Tie strips of rag around the resulting cylinder about 6 inches from each end. Apply glaze to the cylinder's entire surface between the ties with a 2-inch brush, wetting but not saturating the entire surface. The glaze wrinkles the cylinder, producing a surface that will transfer a pattern of streaky lines onto the wall. Have plenty of rags on hand. You can wring out and reuse one roller several times, but the wrinkles will flatten after a while, requiring you to make a new roller.

2 **Glazing the wall.** Divide the wall into imaginary vertical strips about 3 feet wide. Starting at one end of the wall and about two thirds of the way up, set the roller diagonally on the wall and spread your fingers between its ties. Pressing firmly and steadily, walk your fingers atop the cylinder so that it rolls toward the ceiling at a 45° angle; take care not to slide or wipe the rag across the surface. Roll the rag in three adjacent diagonal bands. Then, at the wall's unglazed edges and at any noticeable gaps within the diagonal bands, press the center of the roller against the wall with your thumbs *(right, inset)*. Reload the roller with paint *(Step 1)* and roll the same section of wall diagonally in the opposite direction *(right)*. Roll the remainder of the wall in the same way.

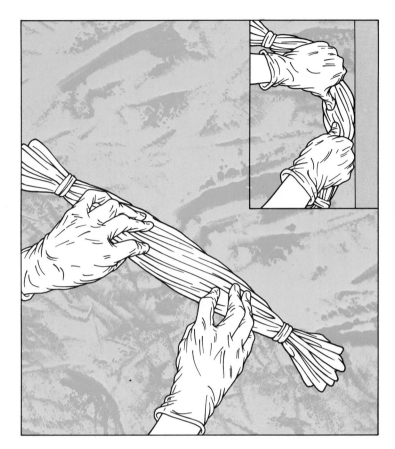

1 **Glazing the edges.** Pour ¼ inch of glaze into a roller pan and dip a textured paint edger into the shallowest portion of the pan. Pat the edger twice on newsprint or butcher's paper to eliminate drips. Then gently set its spacing tabs *(left)* against the ceiling and pat it on the wall with moderate pressure. Glaze the top of the wall from end to end in this manner. Reload the edger with glaze every 2 or 3 feet, and always pat the paper twice before applying glaze to the wall. Then traverse the edge again, this time holding the edger at various angles to the wall's edge.

2 **Rolling the wall.** Load the textured paint roller with glaze *(page 31, top right)*, and push it forward and back for about a foot on a sheet of paper, just once. Starting at the edge of the stippled row near the ceiling, roll a 2-by-3-foot section of wall with back-and-forth strokes in every direction, applying moderate pressure. For a heavier stipple, roll the section a second time *(right)*. Reload the roller with glaze whenever it begins to skip. Cover the remainder of the wall in the same way.

The romantic appeal of hand-crafted stencils

What appears to be wallpaper in the room below turns out, on closer inspection, to be something with much more visual character: a pattern stenciled on the wall by hand. Stenciled borders are not rare (although few have such large, complex designs as the 16-inch-wide border below). But covering entire walls with a stenciled motif, while not uncommon in eras past, is today an unexpected and richly rewarding use of an old craft.

Wallpaper is generally mass-produced and therefore uniform. But subtle differences in the application of paint make each stenciled repeat unique. Wallpaper patterns and colors are limited, whereas you can stencil just about any design you discover or dream up, in any colors you choose. And a wall can be stenciled at a fraction of the cost of wallpaper.

The instructions in Step 1 enable you to make stencil patterns from designs you find in books, copy from textiles or pieces of china, or create in your own imagination. Test the design for scale before making stencil plates. Draw rough sketches of

it in varying sizes (a photocopier that enlarges can make this task easier). Check each size against what decorators call the prominent wall — the one that draws the eye first or most often, such as a wall opposite a sofa or one that gets the most light from a window. If the prominent wall includes a dominant feature, such as the fireplace in this room, test the size in that area. You may decide, for instance, to make a pattern larger to avoid partial repeats between mantelpiece and ceiling. Once the size is determined you can make the plates, mark the necessary reference lines on the wall and apply the paint.

Use japan paints, available in hobby shops; they mix well and dry quickly. To make the plates, buy transparent, 5-mil-thick sheet plastic, frosted on one side to take pencil marks. Get several blunt-ended, stiff-bristled brushes specially made for stencil work (No. 8 brushes are a good choice). And disposable palette sheets, available in art-supply stores, are handy for loading paint on the brushes.

Stenciled designs look best on walls that have a dull, matte finish, and grip better there than on high-gloss surfaces. Clean the backs of stencil plates with a rag dipped in mineral spirits as frequently as necessary. Even plastic plates can wear at the edges of cutouts; for a large project, you may need to make more than one copy of each plate.

1 **Drawing a master pattern.** To create a full-size pattern for the wall design at lower right or the border design at upper right, draw grid lines spaced 1 inch apart on a large sheet of tracing paper. With a pencil, copy the contents of each square shown here into the corresponding square on the tracing paper. Then go over the entire design to make the outlines smooth and fluid. Go over it again with a fine-tipped waterproof marker, for clean, bold tracing lines. Finally, use colored pencils to quickly fill in the approximate color of each part of the design. The white centers of the blossoms seen in the photo at left do not show on the patterns because they are not stenciled, but are added later with a dab of white paint.

The wall pattern here is scaled for a 12-inch-square repeat; the border pattern will be about 16 inches high with an 18-inch running repeat. If you want a larger or smaller pattern, draw on the tracing paper a rectangle the size you want your design to be, and draw evenly spaced grid lines that divide the rectangle into the same number of squares that are shown on the design here. Then copy the contents of each square.

If you are using a design different from the one shown here, start by drawing a grid over it, then proceed as above. ▶

Making Stencil Plates

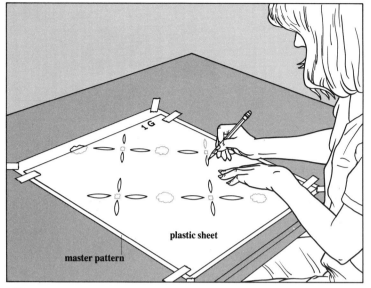

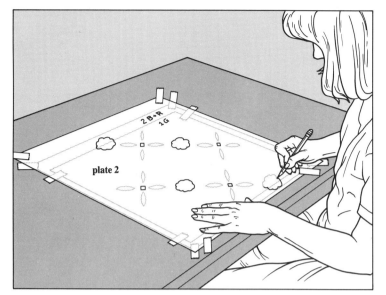

2 Tracing the pattern. Tape the master pattern to a smooth work surface. Lay the plastic sheet for the first plate on top, frosted side up. In most instances, the plastic should extend at least 1½ inches beyond the sketched design on each side. Here, because during stenciling the top edge of the plate will be against the molding that runs below the border, the plastic is positioned so the top edge cuts across the pattern just where the molding will. Pencil the number 1 in the top right corner of the plate, plus the initial letter for the color that will be used with the plate, in this case *G*, for green. Then trace onto the plate all the parts of the pattern that will be painted that color.

3 Tracing the pattern onto the second plate. Tape a second plate, frosted side up, over the first so that its edges extend about 1½ inches beyond the design (including, in this case, the top blossom). Number this plate 2 and label it for the colors to be used with it, here *B* and *R*, for blue and rust; you can use more than one color on a plate so long as the cutouts for different colors are at least 1 inch apart. Trace the appropriate parts of the pattern onto this plate *(above)*. Then, in dashed lines, trace some of the pattern parts near the corners of plate 1 onto plate 2. These will serve as register marks to help you align the stencils on the wall.

Marking the Wall

1 Snapping the first reference line. After you have determined which wall in the room is the most prominent and which feature or area of the wall dominates, find and mark the center point of that feature or area — in this case, the center of the top of the mantel. Fill the chamber of a chalk line *(inset)* with powdered chalk close in color to the wall color. With a helper, use the chalk line to snap a vertical line from the top of the area being stenciled to the center point that you marked below.

4 **Cutting the plates.** Tape the first plate, frosted side up, to a large piece of cardboard that will protect the work surface from cuts. Holding a craft knife like a pencil, cut along a pattern line, pulling the blade toward you. At curves, turn the cutting board rather than the blade, so that you always draw the blade toward you with a steady pressure. Cut out all the outlined areas. If you make a mistake, apply cellophane tape over the unintended slice and cut the shape again. Cut out the pattern parts on the second plate the same way, but do not cut along the dashed register marks. Always use a sharp blade; replace a blade as soon as it starts to dull.

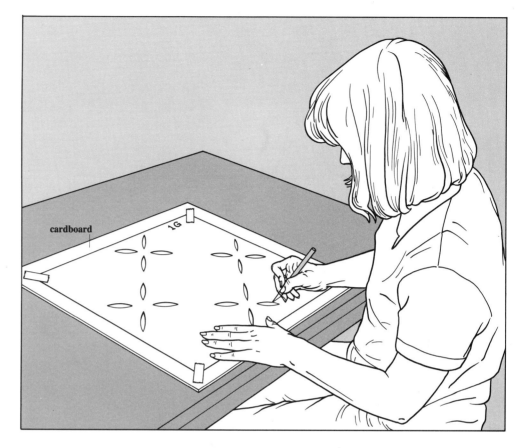

cardboard

2 **Completing the reference lines.** Snap vertical chalk lines along the wall to the right and left of the first line, spacing them the width of the pattern repeat, here 12 inches. Next, snap horizontal lines spaced to the height of each pattern repeat — again, 12 inches here; check these lines with a carpenter's level to make sure they are horizontal. For this pattern, the intersections of the resulting grid indicate the placement of most of the small corner diamonds *(inset)*. So that a full complement of four

leaves will show just below the picture rail, the uppermost horizontal line on this wall is placed 3 inches below the molding.

Snap lines on the other walls the same way. Horizontal lines should flow unbroken around corners. Vertical lines nearest the corner of adjacent walls should be spaced as if the measurement into and out of the corner were on a flat wall.

Stenciling the Main Design

1 **Positioning the first plate.** Place the first plate on the wall so that the appropriate parts of the pattern — here, the top and bottom leaf groupings — are centered on grid-line intersections, as shown above. Then tape the plate to the wall with small strips of masking tape.

2 **Painting the first color.** Pour 1 tablespoon of paint into a pool on a disposable palette sheet, and dip the bristles of the stencil brush into it. Swirl the bristles in a tight circle on a clean part of the palette to remove excess paint. If these swirls stay shiny, the bristles are too wet; swirl the brush again. If the paint dulls immediately, the bristles are correctly loaded for stenciling. Keeping the bristles perpendicular to the wall and moving the brush in small circles, apply the paint through one of the cutouts. For large cutout areas, begin the circling motion from the outside edges and work toward the center. Paint all of the cutouts of the plate. The paint should dry almost immediately. Remove the plate.

5 **Painting the remaining colors.** Starting away from the picture rail so you will not have to bend or cut the second plate immediately, position that plate over a wall section already stenciled with the first plate. Align the dashed-line register marks of the second plate with the painted pattern underneath, and tape the plate in place. Using clean brushes for each different paint, stencil all the cutouts for one color on the plate and then all the cutouts for the other color. Move the plate from position to position, finally stenciling those places that require bending or cutting the plate. Then proceed with a third plate if one is required, and finish the job by adding any necessary nonstenciled touches, such as the white spot painted in the center of each of the blossoms in this design.

3 **Moving the plate.** Reposition the plate lower on the wall so the appropriate parts of the pattern are centered on the next grid-line intersections. Here, the plate's upper leaf group is placed over the lowest already-stenciled leaf group, which serves as register marks (the paint there should already be dry). Tape the plate in place and paint the pattern. Always overlapping a painted pattern as a guide, stencil down the wall and then across it with the first plate. When you are within four plate widths of a baseboard, corner or other obstruction, measure off the remaining repeats to see how the pattern will meet it. You can make fine adjustments if you wish, shifting the plate slightly at each remaining location to change the position of the final pattern by an inch or so.

4 **Stenciling at corners and obstructions.** To stencil across a corner, bend the plate to fit — the plastic is flexible. If cutout portions pucker so paint could leak onto the wall behind the plate, remove the plate and tape it to a work surface. With a straightedge and craft knife, cut it at the line of the bend, then tape the pieces together. Trim away any tape that obscures cutouts and fit the tape-hinged plate back into the corner.

At baseboards, moldings or other obstructions, let the unneeded portion of the plate lap over the obstruction. If the bend causes cutouts to pucker, trim off the unneeded portion.

Stenciling a Border

1 **Cutting the plates.** When dealing with a running border design like this one, where there is no clear separation between pattern repeats, make plates that extend 2 inches beyond the ends of a repeat. Trace the patterns onto those extended portions with dashed lines to serve as register marks, but do not cut them. Trace and cut the pattern repeat itself as you would for a wall stencil (page 53, Step 4). On each plate, draw the lengthwise center line of the pattern, to help you align the pattern properly on the wall.

2 **Painting the design.** Snap a chalk line along the center of the border space and mark the line's center point. Working out from the center point, use a plate to space off repeats and determine where the corners will interrupt the pattern; if you wish, adjust the starting point for a better corner arrangement. Align the center line of the pattern with that of the wall, tape the plate in place and apply the paint (Step 2, opposite). Work first toward one corner and then the other. Repeat the process for additional plates. Bend or cut and tape the plate for corners (Step 4, above). If you encounter an obstruction such as a beam, omit the portion of the pattern that would fill that space. When the job is completed, wipe off chalk marks with a rag and a nonabrasive cleaner.

The wonders of wallpaper

Among the many wall treatments, wallpaper is by far the most diverse in color, pattern and texture. Indeed, the term covers not only paper but also vinyl, fabric, foil, grass-cloth and cork products *(chart, pages 66-67)* that are applied to walls by the same basic paperhanging technique. From a paperhanger's perspective, all these types fit into two categories: those that must be pasted and those that are prepasted *(box, page 58)*.

To determine how many rolls of any type you need, calculate — in feet — the area of each wall, subtracting only for picture windows, French doors and large built-in cabinets. Divide the result by 60, the number of square feet standard American double rolls cover after trimming. Round up any fraction and add a roll for a margin of safety. (If your paper comes in smaller European rolls, ask the dealer for help in estimating your requirements.) The dealer can deliver the requisite amount of wallpaper in double — and sometimes single and triple — rolls. To prevent color variations, order all of your paper at one time so the rolls come from the same press run.

When the paper arrives, have your dealer cut off the selvages, or unpatterned borders, that appear on some rolls. Store the rolls horizontally to protect their fragile edges, and avoid temperatures colder than 42° F., which can crack vinyl papers. Because dealers give refunds (minus a restocking charge) for unopened rolls, hang triple and double rolls first. Before cutting each one, unroll and inspect the entire length; return any damaged paper.

The correct paste type — wheat, cellulose, or vinyl — for your paper is shown on its label and in the chart on pages 66-67. Where alternatives exist, the best choice generally is vinyl paste, which forms a particularly strong bond. Although premixed paste is available, professionals prefer to mix paste from powdered compound. To mix your own paste, buy 1 pound of powder for every seven rolls of paper. Pour the powder into a bucket and slowly beat in warm water with a wire whisk; squeeze out lumps with your fingers. For a medium to thick paste suitable for heavyweight wall coverings, add water only until the whisk stands upright in the paste; for a thin paste suitable for light coverings, add water until the whisk falls over.

Wallpapering requires several specialized but relatively inexpensive tools: a paperhanger's trimming knife and a plentiful supply of blades; a 7-inch paint roller with a medium synthetic nap; a 6-inch broad knife, or taping knife; a smoothing brush with 2-inch bristles; and a seam roller. You also will need a few standard tools: plumb bob with a chalked line, stepladder, metal straightedge, artist's knife, carpenter's level, undyed cellulose sponges, and buckets for paste and water. For a clean, smooth cutting and pasting surface, rent a folding metal 4-by-6-foot paperhanger's table, or cover your worktable with cardboard.

Before papering, switch off power to the room at the service panel: Wet paste can cause short circuits. Remove curtain rods, electric fixtures, stair-rail brackets and other hardware. Mark mounting holes with broken toothpicks that protrude enough to pierce the new paper. If old paper cannot be removed *(box, opposite)* without gouging the wall, fasten loose patches or bubbles with vinyl seam adhesive, spackle uneven areas and sand the entire surface;

How Patterns Match

Widths of patterned wallpaper come either straight-matched or drop-matched. In a straight match *(right, above)*, the pattern's elements are symmetrically arranged. A partial element on one edge of a strip always is placed opposite a matching partial element at the other edge; when two strips meet, the two partial elements join to create a complete element.

In a drop match *(right, below)*, matching partial elements are offset by a regular interval — typically by one row, so that a partial element on one edge is located one row above its complement on the other.

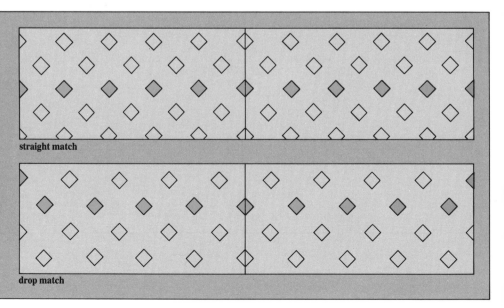

straight match

drop match

then paint it with a vinyl primer-sealer, which also can be used to prepare unpainted drywall or plaster for wallpaper.

Prepare a painted surface for wallpaper as you would for paint *(pages 20-23)*; roughen glossy enamel with medium (100-grit) sandpaper. Paint adjacent ceilings or walls before hanging paper, lapping the paint an inch onto the unpapered wall. Finally, 24 hours in advance, coat the wall with size, transparent sealer that increases new paper's "slip time" and eases its eventual removal; use latex size for most wallpaper, varnish size for fabrics and grass cloth.

Paperhangers traditionally work clockwise around a room, from left to right. At first you may hang only one strip at a time, but as you gain confidence you can cut, paste and hang sets of two or even three strips.

Four tricks can improve the quality of your work:
● Replace your knife blade every four cuts, changing the blade with pliers to avoid cutting your fingers.
● Keep your tools, worktable and newly hung paper spotlessly clean. After pasting each strip, sponge the table; when paste smears, instantly wipe it away. Refill your rinse bucket after every two or three strips.
● Handle paper gently to avoid stretching, scraping or tearing. Adjust with brushes and sponges, not your hands.
● Check each newly hung strip for seam match and bubbles. Sometimes a strip can be straightened by sliding it *(Step 8)*; otherwise, rehang or replace a strip.

Stripping Old Paper

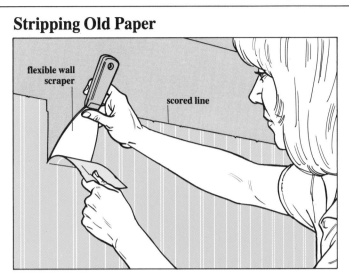

Slip a trimming knife under a top corner of a strip and gently pull down the paper diagonally; if it comes away easily, strip the entire wall similarly. Otherwise, lightly score the wall horizontally and vertically every 4 feet with a sharp trimming knife, changing blades every four cuts. Tape plastic dropcloths to the baseboard and switch off electricity to the room at the service panel. Mix 1 part vinegar and 16 parts warm water in a garden sprayer, and spray the wall with a fine mist until the vinegar solution runs down the wall; repeat this treatment at 20-minute intervals until the paper pulls away easily. With a flexible wall scraper *(above)*, loosen the paper at a scored line and pull it away by hand; scrape only difficult patches. Sponge the stripped wall with vinegar solution.

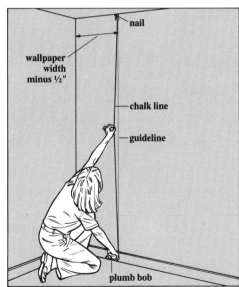

1 **Snapping a guideline.** Subtract ½ inch from the wallpaper's width; near the top, middle and bottom of the wall, make a light pencil mark this distance to the right of the room's least conspicuous corner. Start a nail at the ceiling line, above the mark nearest the corner. Hang a chalked string from the nail to form a plumb line. Hold the string taut at the wall's bottom with one hand, pull the string's center outward a few inches with your other hand and let it snap back sharply *(above)*.

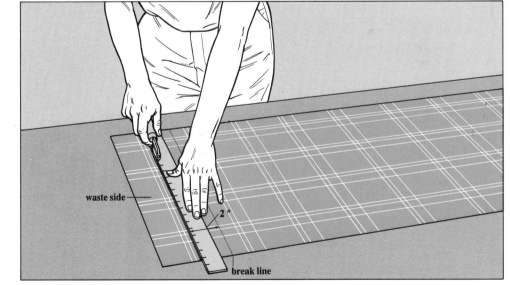

2 **Cutting the first strip.** For wallpaper with a random pattern, vertical stripes or no pattern at all, cut strips 4 inches longer than the height of the wall. For other papers, choose a place to break the pattern at the ceiling line so that none of its elements will be severed. This so-called break line should be at least 2 inches from the roll's end. Mark the break line on the paper's back. Hold a metal yardstick firmly across the face of the paper about 2 inches above the break line and slide a sharp trimming knife lightly along the waste side of the yardstick *(above)*. Then add 2 inches to the wall's height, measure this distance below the break line and cut the paper at this point. ▶

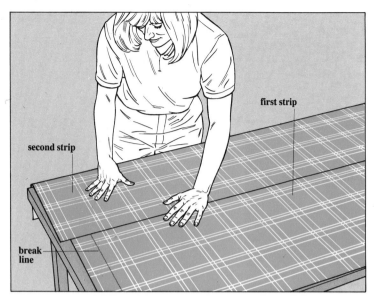

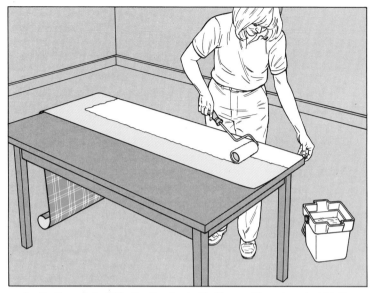

3 **Matching the second strip.** If a pattern needs matching, unroll beside the first strip a second one from the same roll; match the pattern at the strips' tops and measure the excess on the new strip. Unroll a strip from a second roll and measure the excess; using the alternate roll may reduce waste. Mark the break line on the strip with less waste and cut this strip to length, taking the first one as a guide. Number the strips. Change your knife blade, then measure, cut and number two more strips. Let the last three strips roll up naturally and set them aside.

For paper that does not have a pattern to match, cut three strips to the length of the first one *(Step 1)*.

4 **Pasting a strip.** Fill a 2-gallon bucket halfway with paste and whisk the paste until it is smooth. Loosely roll the first strip, pattern facing inward, taking care not to crease the paper; unroll the strip on a work surface, pattern down. Submerge a 7-inch paint roller in paste, then hold the roller above the paste and spin it slowly to release excess paste. Align a corner of the strip with one of the surface's corners. Hold down the corner with your thumb and roll a thick film of paste onto the quarter of the strip nearest you *(above)*; spread paste flush with the strip's edge and to within 1 inch of its end. At the same end, align the unpasted corner with the matching corner of the work surface and paste the adjacent quarter.

Preparing Prepasted Paper

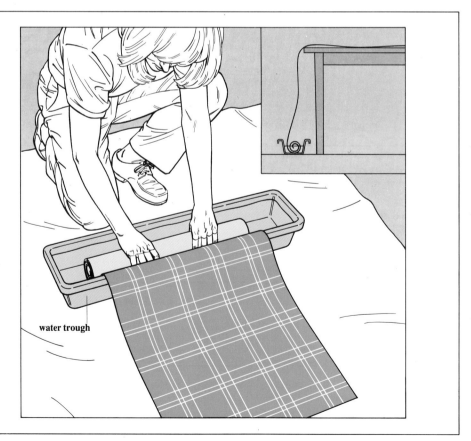

Place a plastic water trough two thirds full of warm water on a dropcloth at the foot of a worktable. If the table's edge is rough or sharp, put masking tape over it.

Unroll the wallpaper strip, pattern facing up, on the floor; slide the end into the water, then roll up the strip *(right)*, taking care not to crease it. If the strip will not remain submerged, weight it with an old screwdriver — a heavy weight might crush it.

Leave the paper submerged for the time recommended by the manufacturer — usually 60 seconds, but no more than three minutes. Then lift the strip slowly by its top corners, letting water drain back into the trough, and slide the strip's face onto the table *(inset)*. Book the strip *(Step 5)* and hang it within 30 minutes.

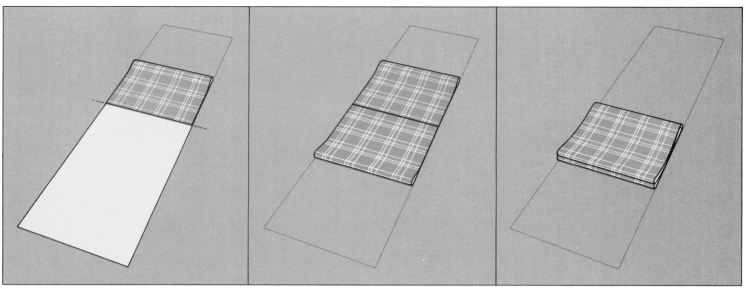

5 **Booking a strip.** Grasp the corners of the pasted half of the strip and set the pasted end against the strip's midline, with the pasted sides facing each other and the edges aligned *(above, left)*. Take care not to crease the strip at the fold. Slide the folded end off the worktable. Paste the strip's two remaining quarters *(Step 4)* and fold them, bringing the newly pasted end beside the first one *(above, center)*. Fold one of the strip's two halves over the other *(above, right)*. Set the strip aside. Wipe the worktable with a damp sponge.

Paste and book two more strips, reserving the fourth as a cutting guide for succeeding strips. Let the paper absorb the paste for at least 10 minutes, but always hang a strip within 60 minutes of applying the paste.

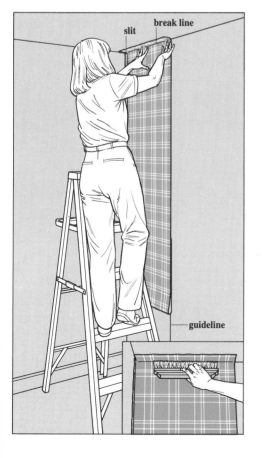

6 **Starting the first strip.** Open the strip as far as the pasted folds. Grasp the top corners and peel apart the top fold. Align the break line with the ceiling line and the right edge with the guideline; pat the strip's top to the wall *(left)* and corner. Use a trimming knife to slit the top corner vertically to the ceiling line; pat the paper onto the side wall. Push the bristles of a smoothing brush against the ceiling line *(inset)*. Then, starting midway on the top half, lightly brush the paper outward from its center. Finally, tap the brush into the corner to smooth the side wall.

7 **Finishing the strip.** Grasp the corners of the strip's bottom end and gently peel apart the pasted layers *(right)*. Pat the strip onto the wall; at the corner, vertically slit the paper from the bottom exactly to the baseboard's top. Brush the strip's bottom half outward from the center. Then brush the whole strip from top to bottom with long vertical strokes. Ignore small bubbles and wrinkles, which usually disappear as paste dries. But if a bubble more than 2 inches in diameter cannot be brushed out, gently lift the corner nearest the bubble to release it, then brush the strip back into place. ▶

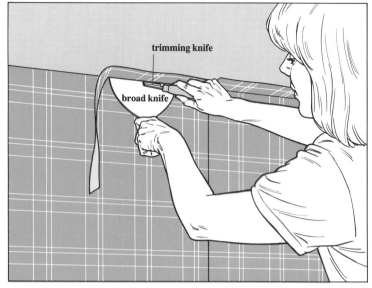

8 **Hanging the second strip.** Press the top of the second strip temporarily to the wall with your thumbs and align the new strip's pattern with the old one's. Butt the edges of the strips tightly so they meet in a tiny ridge that juts out about 1/16 inch from the wall; then hang the strip *(Steps 6 and 7)*. The ridge of the butt joint will disappear as the paste dries. If the edges do not butt along their entire length, press a pair of dampened sponges about 4 inches to each side of the open seam. Slide and stretch both strips until their edges meet. Get off the ladder and recheck the pattern's match; if any mismatch cannot be corrected with sponges, immediately pull the new strip slowly off the wall from its bottom to within 6 inches of the top and realign it.

9 **Trimming the strips.** Working from top to bottom, retighten the first strip by pressing a nearly dry sponge into the corners at the top, bottom and side. Then place the edge of the blade of a 6-inch broad knife over the first strip along the ceiling line at the corner. Hold a trimming knife above the broad knife at a 60° angle to the wall and slide its blade lightly along that of the broad knife; when you reach the broad knife's end, leave the trimming knife against the wall, move the broad knife forward and resume the cut. When you finish trimming both strips at the ceiling, replace the knife blade with a new one. Trim along the baseboard, placing the trimming knife below the broad knife. Immediately put trimmings in a plastic bag; they are a hazard underfoot.

Wrapping a Cover Plate

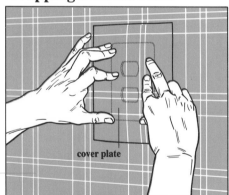

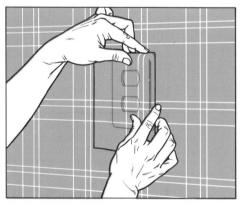

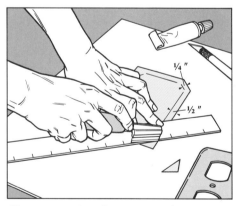

1 **Matching.** Cut an unpasted scrap of wallpaper several inches larger than the cover plate, making sure that the scrap's pattern will match the paper around the electric box. Hold the plate over its switch or outlet, and slide the wallpaper piece over the plate, matching its pattern to the already-papered wall on all sides; center the paper to minimize the tiny, inevitable mismatch created by the raised plate.

2 **Creasing.** Ease the plate's top away from the wall and fold the paper sharply over the top edge. Still maintaining the paper's alignment, pull the plate's side away from the wall and fold the paper around it. Then crease the paper around the remaining edges. Put the paper face down on a work surface; cut 1/2 inch outside each crease, using a straightedge and a trimming knife.

3 **Trimming.** Cut off each corner of paper at a 45° angle 1/4 inch outside the plate's corner. Smear a thin film of seam adhesive over the front of the plate with your finger. Let the adhesive set for two minutes, then put the paper on the plate and fold under its edges. After the adhesive dries for an hour, put the plate face down and cut along its inner openings with an artist's knife.

10 **Cleaning the paper.** Wet a sponge in warm water and wring it almost dry. Lightly wipe all paste from the wallpaper, ceiling and woodwork; do not rub the paper. Refill the bucket with clean water after sponging every two strips. If the next day you discover patches of dry paste, a solution of 1 tablespoon of trisodium phosphate to 1 gallon of water will remove them — but test a scrap first to be sure the paper's colors are fast.

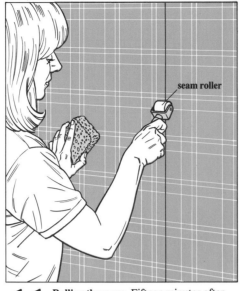

seam roller

11 **Rolling the seam.** Fifteen minutes after hanging the second strip, set a seam roller at the seam's center. Using long, light up-and-down strokes, roll to the ceiling line; keep both the roller and seam clean with a sponge. Roll the lower half of the seam similarly. Lift any seam that opens the next day with a trimming knife, squeeze in vinyl seam adhesive, spread it with a finger and let it set for two minutes; roll the seam and wipe it at once.

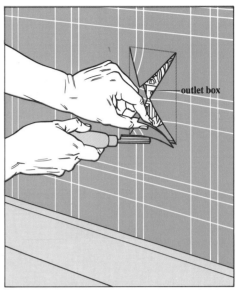

outlet box

12 **Trimming for electric boxes.** Turn off the electricity to the room at the main switch and remove the plate covering the box of an outlet, switch or fixture. Hang wallpaper over the box *(Steps 6 and 7)*. Cut an X in the strip just large enough to accommodate any protruding elements. Brush and trim the strip, then extend the X to the box's corners and cut along its inside edges *(above)*. Pull away the wallpaper scraps and wipe up the paste.

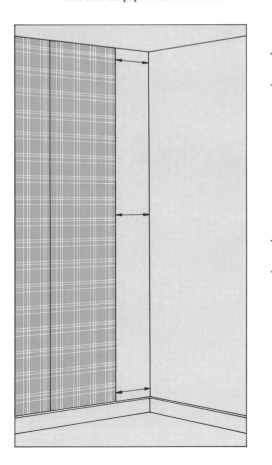

13 **Turning an inside corner.** When you are less than a full strip from an inside corner, measure between the corner and the top, middle and bottom of the last full strip *(arrows, left)*. Add ½ inch to the longest measurement. If the sum is less than 4 inches, proceed to Step 14. If the sum is within 4 inches of a full strip's width, hang a full strip around the corner; press its crease into the corner with a smoothing brush. If the sum falls between these extremes, cut a full strip vertically to make a left section as wide as the sum, and hang it in the usual way.

14 **Snapping a new guideline.** If you did not hang a strip in Step 13, subtract from a full strip's width ½ inch plus the distance from the last strip to the corner. Mark this measure from the corner at the middle of the new wall, and snap a line at the mark. Hang a full strip around the corner, setting its right edge on the line.

If you hung a partial strip in Step 13 *(drawing at right),* subtract ½ inch from the width of the leftover strip; if you hung a full strip, subtract ½ inch from a full width. Midwall, mark this distance from the last strip. Snap a chalk line at the mark and hang the next partial or full strip. ▶

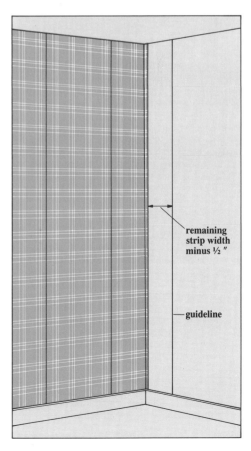

remaining strip width minus ½ "

guideline

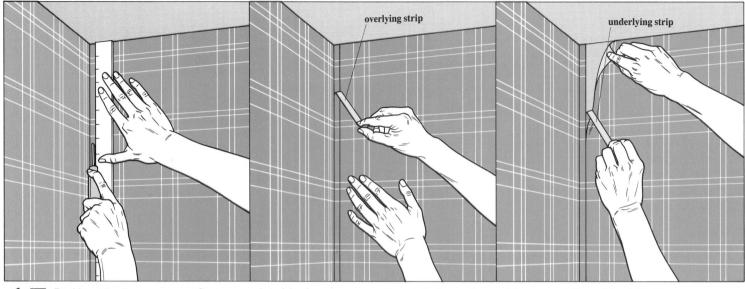

15 **Double-cutting the corner seam.** Center a metal straightedge on the overlapped seam at the wall's top corner. Hold the straightedge firmly against the wall.

Draw a trimming knife smoothly down along the straightedge *(above, left);* bear down moderately on the knife blade, holding the blade tight against the straightedge and never lifting it away from the cut. Peel away the overlying severed sliver of the right strip *(above, center)* and cut it off midway down the wall.

Gently lift the right strip's remaining edge with the flat of the trimming knife. Peel away the underlying sliver of the left strip *(above, right)* and cut it off. Roll the top portion of the seam *(Step 11),* then cut and roll the lower portions in the same way.

Turning an Outside Corner

Most outside corners are approximately plumb — check yours with a carpenter's level *(inset)* to be sure the level's bubble remains within the outer lines scribed on its vial — and do not require snapping a new guideline on the second wall. Even if the corner is not plumb, hang a strip of paper around it before making corrections.

Unless the last strip ends within ½ inch of the corner, hang a full strip around the corner. Apply the strip's left side to the left wall and brush the paper smooth. Then slit the strip's top and bottom at the corner and apply the strip to the right wall. Use a seam roller *(right)* to smooth the corner.

Check the right-hand edge of the strip with the level at three heights. If the corner is plumb and this edge is not, lift the strip off the right wall and press a damp sponge repeatedly onto the left wall, working toward the corner to remove bubbles, which commonly cause misalignment.

If the last strip ends within ½ inch of the corner or if a new strip extends less than ½ inch beyond the corner, subtract 1 inch from a strip's width. Snap a line this distance from the corner, set a new strip on the line and double-cut the seam *(Step 15)* as far left of the corner as possible.

If the corner itself is not plumb, measure to the right of the new corner strip the width of a strip minus ½ inch; snap a vertical guideline at the mark and align the next strip with the line, then double-cut the overlapping seam.

Accommodating a Framed Opening

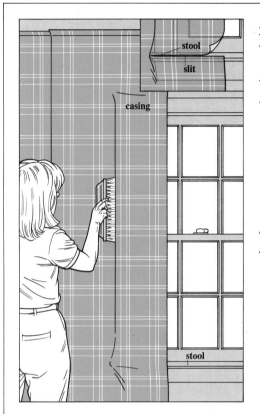

1 **Starting the opening.** Hang a full strip that overlaps the left edge of the door or window. Brush the strip from its left edge toward the obstruction (*left*).

On a window with an inner sill or stool, brush the strip to the casing and the end of the stool. Slit the paper horizontally along the side and front edges of the stool (*inset*). Use an artist's knife to trim the paper along the end of the stool, then pat and brush the strip around it.

2 **Completing the opening.** Remove all but 2 inches of overlap, then make diagonal slits from the paper's corners to the corners of the casing. Smooth the paper above the opening (and below it, for a window). Trim the paper around the casing (*page 60, Step 9*). Fit a partial strip above — and, for a window, below — the casing. On the opening's right edge, brush a full strip down to the top molding. Cut the overlap and make a diagonal slit at the corner, then fit and smooth the strip at the side of the window. Cut the remaining side overlaps, slit the corner and finish the bottom of the strip.

Working Around a Recessed Window

Hang a strip taut over the opening and trim it at the ceiling line and baseboard (*page 60, Step 9*). Use scissors to make a horizontal cut across the middle of the opening, stopping 1 inch from the side; then cut vertically 1 inch from the side and end, with a 45° diagonal cut to the corner (*above, left*). Cut the bottom half of the paper similarly. Press the three resulting flaps onto the matching walls of the window well and trim them at the window in the usual way (*above, center*).

To cover the window's side wall, cut a piece of paper 6 inches longer than the side wall and ½ inch wider, matching its pattern to the adjacent wall. Hang and trim this piece (*above, right*), then double-cut the three overlapping seams along the left, top and bottom of the piece. Angle the cuts at the corners so that no gaps occur there. Paper the remainder of the window well in the same way.

Papering a Ceiling

Starting at the short wall opposite the room's main entrance, measure the ceiling width and make tick marks at a distance from each corner equal to the width of a wallpaper strip minus ½ inch. Snap a guideline between the marks *(page 57, Step 1)*. Cut and paste several strips the full ceiling width plus 2 inches extra at each end for trim; match the pattern as you proceed. Fold each pasted strip creaselessly at approximately 12-inch intervals, putting pasted faces together accordion fashion.

Set two stepladders at the ends of the wall and suspend a 2-by-10 scaffold plank between them; use a double thickness of 2-by-10s for distances greater than 6 feet.

While a helper holds the folded paper, align its edge with the guideline and allow 2 inches of its end to drop onto the long wall. Cut out a ½-by-2-inch rectangle at the ceiling corner *(inset)*. Pat and brush 2-foot sections onto the ceiling, walking backward along the plank. Cut out a rectangle at the ceiling corner at the end of the strip, then brush the paper into the corner and rebrush the strip's entire length.

Hang the remaining strips similarly. If you plan to paper the walls, wait until you paper each one to double-cut *(page 62, Step 15)* a seam just below the ceiling line; otherwise, trim the ceiling paper in the ordinary way *(page 60, Step 9)*.

Papering a Stairwell

After papering an upper landing, set up a scaffold with a stepladder, an extension ladder and planks *(page 37)*. Hang strips on the well wall from the scaffold in the usual way, measuring and cutting each strip separately so it is long enough to reach from the ceiling to the lowest step it must meet. Get off the scaffold after each strip, push the extension ladder away from the wall, brush down the bottom of the strip and trim the paper at the baseboard.

When you have hung the last full-width strip before the corner of the head wall, measure to the head wall at three points and add ½ inch to the largest measure; cut and hang a strip this wide, letting it overlap the head wall. Slit it at the top and bottom of the head wall. Snap a guideline on the head wall at a distance from the well wall equal to the width of the remaining partial strip minus ½ inch. Cut the rest of the head-wall strips 4 inches longer than its height. Paste the strips; pat, brush and trim the top half of each one. Disassemble the scaffold, move the stepladder to the lower landing and lay the planks from the ladder to a stair tread. Brush the lower half of each head-wall strip, wrapping the overlap onto the lower landing's ceiling if you plan to paper it; otherwise, trim the strips ⅟₁₆ inch above the bottom of the wall. Paper the second well wall if you have one.

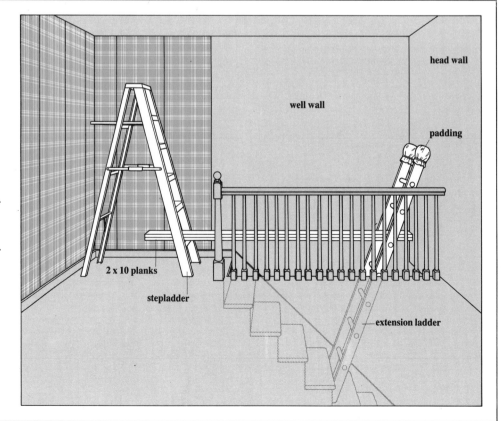

Papering a Dormered Room

The numbers on the drawing at right show the correct sequence in which to paper a dormered room: Paper the main room's ceiling (1), then its sloped walls (2) and knee walls (3) before its other vertical walls (4). For dormers and other alcoves, paper the ceiling (5), the vertical walls (6) and finally the triangular wall segments (7).

To paper a sloped wall, begin by holding the first strip at the ceiling line and matching its pattern and seam to that on the ceiling. Mark its break line on the paper's back. Mark the sloped wall just below the ceiling line along the paper's right edge; make a matching mark at the sloped wall's bottom and snap a guideline between the marks.

Match, cut, paste and hang the first strip as you would on a vertical wall, leaving a 2-inch overlap onto the knee wall and cutting out rectangles at the top and bottom left-hand corners of the strip so its overlap onto the side wall lies flat (inset).

Beside the dormer in the sloped wall, hang a full strip that overlaps the opening, then with scissors cut away all but 1 inch of overlap. Make a diagonal slit at the corner and fold the overlapping edges into the dormer. Paper above the opening, then hang an overlapping strip on its right side.

After completing the sloped wall, hang the first knee-wall strip below the first strip on the slope. Match the seams and pattern. Double-cut the seams just below the sloped wall when you complete the knee wall.

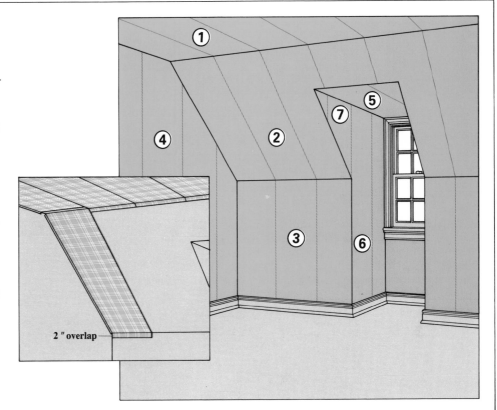

2 " overlap

Hanging Lining Paper

An underlayer of lining paper will prepare rough or damaged surfaces for wallpaper and provide a backing for fragile papers (chart, pages 66-67). Lining paper is unprinted — and uncolored — and has a nap surface that readily absorbs size, paste or paint. It is available in various widths. Lining paper comes in light to heavy weights, including paper reinforced with fiber or backed with cloth to smooth a surface as rough as concrete blocks.

Apply lining paper horizontally. Cut the strips as long as the unobstructed sections of walls and fold them accordion fashion (opposite, top), if you have a helper. Otherwise, cut the strips into lengths of about 4 feet — irregular enough so the ends do not line up vertically when you hang them — and book them in the usual way. In either case, use the same adhesive for the lining paper as you will use for the final wall covering. Hang the first strip with one edge along the ceiling line. Butt each subsequent strip, working toward the baseboard. Where seams cannot be butted, leave gaps up to ⅛ inch wide, or overlap the edges and double-cut them (page 62, Step 15).

Trim the paper flush with window and door casings, corners and baseboards. Wait 24 hours, apply size to the lining paper and let it set for 24 hours, then hang the wallpaper.

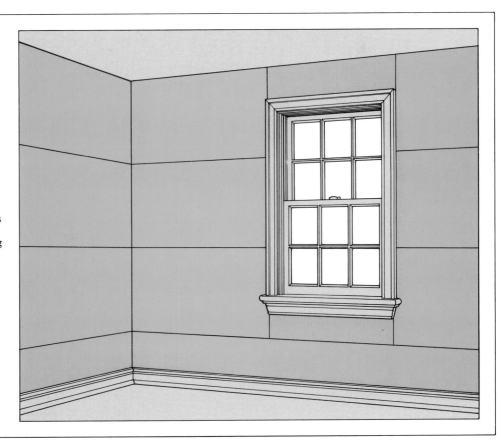

Choosing the right wall covering

Apart from the myriad colors and patterns available in wall coverings, the decorator also is presented with an endless array of materials, textures and specialized finishes. To make your choice of pattern easier when you go to buy, narrow your selection beforehand to those wall coverings best suited to the room's use and the condition of the walls. This chart lists the major types of wall coverings available, together with information on how they are sold, applied and cared for. Unusual materials such as heavy-duty, extra-wide vinyls and fragile, random-width veneers require special handling as noted, but generally most of the coverings can be hung by the methods described on pages 56-65.

The most popular and universally used coverings are the common papers, which include machine- and hand-printed papers in a wide range of sizes, with or without pretrimmed edges. Machine prints may have unpasted or prepasted backings, may be untreated or stain-resistant, or have vinyl-coated surfaces.

While many common papers are a good deal tougher and more washable than those made a generation ago, none can match the scuff resistance and scrubbability of the coverings grouped under the heading "vinyls." These materials stand up well to water, grease, fingerprints, and a certain amount of abrasion. The remainder of the wall coverings listed are somewhat more specialized in their application, but each has sterling qualities that make it ideal in particular locations.

Note, too, that each kind of wall covering has a recommended adhesive. Vinyl films, for example, do not breathe and therefore require a premixed fungicidal adhesive that will deter the growth of mold between wall and backing.

One other feature that the home decorator should consider in choosing a covering is how easy it will be to strip. People who rent their dwellings and whose leases stipulate that walls must be returned to their original condition would be wise to select a covering that can be removed easily or, if not, put a removable lining paper (page 65) or a strippable-release primer-sealer underneath. Lining papers also help ensure that specialized coverings, such as foils, hang smooth and flat.

A Chart of Comparative Characteristics

Type	How Sold
Common Papers Untreated Vinyl-coated Cloth-backed	Double rolls, with some single and triple rolls. Widths and lengths vary, but 27 inches is common for American paper. A double roll holds 72 square feet and covers 60 square feet after trimming. "Eurorolls" are generally smaller. Read the labels carefully.
Vinyls Paper-backed Fabric-backed Foam-backed	Same as common papers; heavy commercial grades also available in widths to 54 inches and lengths to approximately 30 yards.
Metallics Paper-backed foil Fabric-backed foil Paper-backed simulated metal Fabric-backed simulated metal	Same as common papers.
Flocks On paper On vinyl-coated paper On fabric-backed vinyl	Same as common papers.
Fabrics Unbacked Paper-backed	Bolts usually 45 inches wide, but also in widths of 36, 54 and 60 inches; sold usually by the linear yard.
Felt Paper-backed	Bolts 54 inches wide; sold by the linear or square yard.
Special Textures Grass cloth, paper-backed Burlap, paper- or fabric-backed Strings, fabric-backed Synthetic suede, fabric-backed Synthetic leather, fabric-backed	Double rolls, 36 inches wide and 24 feet long.
Cork Paper-backed	Usually 36 inches wide, 24 feet long.
Embossed Papers Linoleum-like relief on paper (Lincrusta®) Double-thickness paper, plain or vinyl-coated (Anaglypta®) Cotton-fiber paper (Supaglypta®)	Same as common papers.
Wood Veneers Fabric-backed random wood-grain patterns Fabric-backed matched wood-grain veneers	Strips 10 to 24 inches wide and up to 12 feet long; end-matched strips for taller walls available on request. (Each strip is called a bent.)

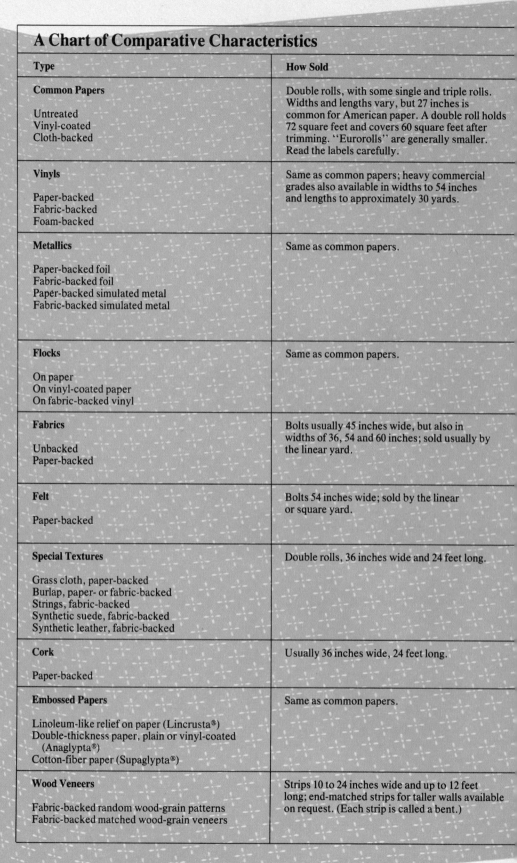

Adhesives	Special Handling Hints	Wear and Care
Wheat or cellulose paste. Prepasted papers have factory-applied, water-activated adhesive — generally wheat paste.	Treat carefully to avoid rips. If vinyl-coated, double-cut unavoidable overlaps (*page 62, Step15*) or use vinyl seam adhesive at overlaps to make vinyl adhere to vinyl.	Appropriate in areas of moderate wear, such as dining rooms and adult bedrooms. Susceptible to grease stains and abrasions. Many pattern inks run if wetted; test a corner before attempting to wash. Dust with soft mop or use vacuum cleaner.
Mildew-resistant type; premixed vinyl paste suggested except for prepasted vinyls.	Double-cut unavoidable overlaps (*page 62, Step 15*) or use vinyl seam adhesive at overlaps to make vinyl adhere to vinyl.	Most durable type currently available, especially recommended for kitchens, baths, halls and children's rooms. Almost always strippable. Can be washed with mild detergent solution.
Premixed vinyl paste except for pre-pasted foils.	Hang lining paper (*page 65*) over rough walls. Coat smooth walls with oil-based primer-sealer, then put paste on walls — not covering — applying it in widths slightly wider than the covering. Wrinkles cannot be erased; smooth only with soft brush; roll seams lightly. Foils conduct electricity: Turn off power to room and cut foil cleanly around electric outlets.	Dramatic in small areas, such as baths, alcoves or hallways. Fragile and hard to handle; can cause glare in sunny areas; can show dents. Can be washed with mild detergent solution.
Same pastes as for other common papers, vinyls or metallics, but slightly thicker mixtures to handle weight and greater stiffness.	Vacuum loose flock particles from back before applying adhesive. Never use a seam roller to press down seams: Gently tap them flat with the edge of a smoothing brush.	Paper flocks best reserved for formal areas, such as dining rooms or halls; vinyl types popular in children's rooms. Most flocks should be vacuum cleaned, but prepasted types can be washed with mild detergent solution.
Heavy-duty clear-drying premixed paste for both unbacked and paper-backed.	Unbacked fabric must be preshrunk. Hang over lining paper (*page 65*); stretch covering until taut, but do not pull fabric out of shape. Hang first sheet between two plumb lines and subsequent sheets between a seam and a plumb line.	Help to absorb and deaden sound. Good choices for areas of moderate wear, such as dining rooms and adult bedrooms. Soil easily but can be cleaned with dry-cleaning fluids or powders.
Heavy-duty clear-drying premixed vinyl paste.	Hang over lining paper (*page 65*). Position strips with nap in same direction. Avoid paste smears, which can cause puckering and fading.	Absorbs and deadens sound. Recommended for areas of moderate wear. Some colors tend to fade, so avoid walls in full sun. Can be vacuum cleaned, but stains are hard to remove.
Heavy-duty clear-drying premixed paste.	If shading appears at seams, reverse every other strip top for bottom to prevent abrupt changes of shading. Hang over lining paper (*page 65*).	Decorative choices for areas of moderate wear, such as living and dining rooms. All available in either natural or synthetic fibers. Susceptible to soil; dust with soft mop or use vacuum cleaner.
Any adhesive except heavy-duty clay-based premixed paste.	Hang over lining paper (*page 65*). Edges are fragile and break unless handled with extra care.	Helps to absorb and deaden sound, so especially welcome in recreation rooms, children's rooms or studies. Can be vacuum cleaned or washed.
Vinyl-to-vinyl paste for Lincrusta® paper; heavy-duty vinyl paste for all others.	Soaking for 10 to 15 minutes necessary after pasting and booking to make covering supple. (Oversoaking, however, may cause delamination.) Seam roller will crush pattern; smooth seams with a brush.	Distinctive covering for walls that will not require frequent washing. Often used to mask cracked, irregular walls. Sold only in white or natural, but can be painted, enameled or varnished as desired after it has hung for 36 hours. Dust with soft mop or use vacuum cleaner.
Special contact adhesive of type specified and provided by manufacturer.	Edges are fragile and break unless handled with great care; do not book or fold after applying paste; set room temperature to 70° F. or higher for fast drying; use manufacturer's recommended sequence when hanging matched veneers.	Gives effect of wood paneling at less cost. Fire-resistant. Needs to be finished like other woods (pages 84-85). Cannot be repositioned once placed on the wall. Can be dusted or vacuum cleaned.

Defining a room with borders

Wallpaper borders are a quick and inexpensive way to add distinction to a plain room or to accentuate handsome architectural details in a more lavishly endowed one. They can be used alone, or in conjunction with wallpapers. Areas that especially invite these decorative strips include the tops and bottoms of walls, the perimeters of windows and doors, the edges of staircases and stairwells, and across walls at chair- or plate-rail height — 30 to 36 inches from the floor for chair rails and 60 inches from the floor for plate rails. The only major restriction regarding the use of borders is that the lines along which they run must be straight: Pasting a border under an uneven ceiling line, for example, merely calls unnecessary attention to the irregularity.

Borders are available by the linear foot at wallpaper stores and are often accompanied by related paper and fabric. They may be vinyl or paper, prepasted or plain, and are installed with standard wallpaper adhesives and tools (*pages 57-62*).

To estimate how much material you need, measure the paths the borders will take and total the results. Allow extra for trimming at the ends and mitering overlaps at corners of windows and doors.

Most borders are applied by butting one side against a ceiling line or the edge of a molding. For chair and plate rails, measure the required distance from the floor and snap a chalk line (*page 57, Step 1*) as a guide for the bottom of the border. At windows and doors, hold the border against the top and side casings, and mark the outside edges of the corners.

A parade of fanciful animals brightens a related nursery wallpaper.

Bold S curves underscore the rise of a staircase.

Shaded and shaped edges enhance the illusion of draped fabric in this simulated swag.

Bands of brilliant green enliven a plain window.

Swarms of butterflies rim the ceiling and pass-through with color.

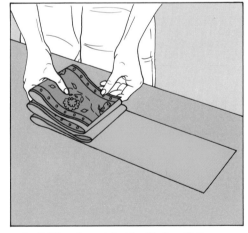

1 **Folding the pasted strip.** Mark guidelines for the border on the wall, if necessary. Unroll the border — pattern side up — on a worktable, and use a utility knife and a straightedge to first square and then cut a strip of the required length, but not to exceed 3 or 4 feet. Apply paste *(page 58, Step 4),* then fold the strip at 6-inch intervals, alternating the direction of the folds accordion-fashion so that the pasted sides face each other. Do not crease the folds.

2 **Applying the border.** Align the side of the strip with the adjacent guideline or molding. Holding the strip in one hand, gently press the pasted side to the wall with your other hand, one 6-inch section at a time. Keep a sponge handy to wipe up any errant drops of paste before they harden. Use a smoothing brush to remove any wrinkles or bubbles in the paper.

3 **Mitering corners.** Leave unpasted a final section equal to the strip's width. Similarly, leave an unpasted section at the start of the next strip. Install the two strips, letting the unpasted sections overlap and adjusting the overlap so the pattern matches. Holding a straightedge between the inside and outside corners of the overlapping pieces, cut through them both with a utility knife. Lift away the loose triangles and paste the mitered ends to the wall.

Adding texture with textile

Textiles on walls soften a room's geometry and offer intricacies of texture, pattern and color that cannot be achieved with most paints or wallpapers. For these reasons — and because cloth can hide surface damage — fabric is sometimes used to cover entire walls *(pages 72-79)*.

More frequently, decorative textile pieces are hung like paintings. Be they rugs, tapestries, batiks or patchwork quilts, wall hangings must be displayed with care if they are to last. They must be protected from direct sunlight and strong artificial light, which will fade the colors and weaken fibers. Excessive moisture can cause mildew, and excessive aridity can lead to brittle and broken fibers.

Most important, they must have evenly distributed support — at the very least, all the way across the top of the piece. Never hang a textile that you care about with pushpins, nails or tacks; they may tear the fabric and almost certainly will give it a scalloped edge. And do not add a rod or other weight to the bottom to make the textile hang flat; the stress can damage the piece.

Any of the three basic hanging methods shown here can be used with any type of textile. However, it is advisable to consult a professional textile conservationist (a museum is a good place to start looking for one) if you are dealing with a particularly fragile or valuable piece.

When attaching a textile to a cloth backing, sew by hand through all of the layers of fabric to the piece's front surface; you can conceal the stitches by placing them in seams or design lines and using matching colors. Choose thread that is 100 per cent cotton — silk if the textile is made of silk — and use a double strand if the textile is heavy.

For mounting, backing and casing fabrics, use only washed unbleached muslin or washed undyed cotton flannel, choosing a weight compatible with that of the textile. The cotton webbing used in the Velcro® hanging method *(opposite, top)* can be obtained from an upholstery supplier. Seal all wood with polyurethane varnish to prevent saps and acids from bleeding onto the textile. The most suitable woods are poplar and clear sugar pine. Needles, staples and any other metal used should be rustproof.

Rod and lining. Muslin lining with a sleevelike casing at the top makes it easy to suspend a quilt — or rug or other textile — from a rod. Stitched to the quilt at many points, the lining provides fairly even support while protecting the back of the piece from dust and abrasion.

The lining fabric is cut to extend 2 inches beyond each side of the quilt and 3 inches beyond the top and bottom (you may have to sew several widths of fabric together). The sides and bottom of the lining are folded and machine-stitched into hems with the raw edges turned under ½ inch; the hems are made just wide enough so that the finished lining edges fall ½ inch inside the edges of the quilt. The casing is made the same way except that it is folded to the outer side of the lining.

The lining is sewed to the quilt by hand with a ½-inch running stitch just above the bottom hem and along both long sides of the casing, and with separate, knotted tacking stitches at intervals over the whole surface — the heavier the textile, the more tacking stitches needed. Stitches should be placed along the quilt's design lines or seams and should pass all the way through all layers to the front surface. Slits are cut in the back of the casing for the L hooks that support the rod, a standard closet pole sealed with polyurethane varnish.

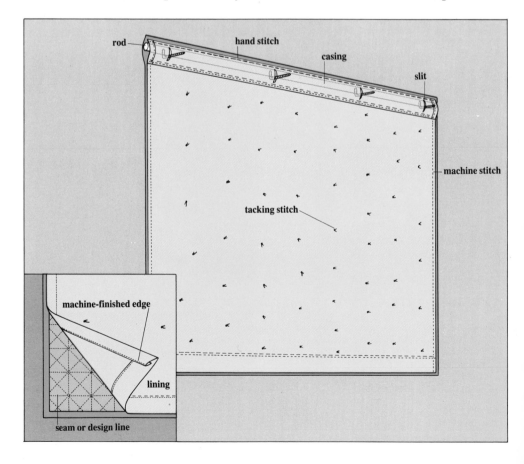

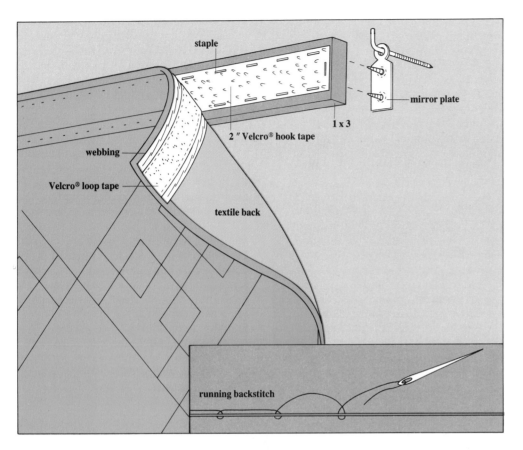

Velcro® tape and board. This combination offers ample support for a quilt or other textile in good condition. Two-inch-wide Velcro® gripping tape and 3-inch-wide undyed cotton webbing are cut ½ inch shorter than the top width of the textile piece being displayed. The loop portion of the Velcro® tape is machine-stitched to the lengthwise center of the webbing. Then the webbing is hand-sewed to the back of the textile just below the top edge: Use a 1-inch running backstitch *(inset)* and work from the center of the webbing out to the ends.

The hook portion of the Velcro® tape is stapled onto a polyurethane-sealed 1-by-3 so that the tape is the same distance from the top of the board as the Velcro® loop tape is from the top of the textile. Depending on the weight of the textile, two, three or more mirror plates are evenly spaced across the back of the board. (Screw eyes driven into the top edge of the board can be used instead.)

Attach the textile to the board before lifting the board onto L hooks or other hangers on the wall. This technique will subject the piece to less stress than if you attach it to an already-mounted board.

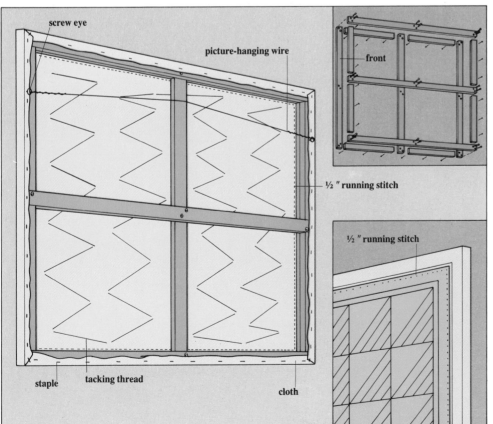

Fabric stretched on a frame. One of the most attractive and most protective ways to display a cherished textile object is to sew it to cloth stretched on a custom-fitted frame. The piece is kept flat, wrinkle-free and shielded from the wall, and its weight is evenly distributed, with no concentrations of stress.

This frame extends 3¼ inches beyond each edge of the textile. It is constructed of two layers of polyurethane-sealed 1-by-3s assembled as shown in the upper inset; the longer boards are cut to the length and width desired for the frame and the smaller ones are sized to fill the spaces between them. The boards are held together with yellow carpenter's glue, 1¼-inch No. 8 flathead screws and 1¼-inch brads.

Washed cotton flannel or muslin is stretched tight over the frame and stapled. The corners are miter-folded. The textile is pinned in place, then hand-sewed to the cloth with a ½-inch running stitch around the textile's edges. Tacking stitches along seam or design lines fix the central portion of the textile to the cloth. The frame can be hung like a picture on wire strung between two screw eyes, or suspended from mirror plates like those used on the board above.

Rich folds fitted between rods

Fabric gathered — or shirred — on wall-mounted curtain rods can be a handsome and practical alternative to paint or wallpaper. Cloth has excellent acoustical properties, provides good insulation and, if the wall is damaged, requires no time-consuming pre-installation repair work.

The ⅜-inch round steel rods, bought from a drapery-supply dealer in 12-foot lengths and cut to fit at home *(Step 1)*, are supported by barrel brackets. The shirred fabric panels they hold are nothing more than large curtains with a rod casing and a 2-inch gathered heading at the bottom as well as at the top. It is not even necessary to sew lengths of fabric together into panels. Instead, you can hang individual pieces of fabric with the selvages left on, simply casing them at top and bottom; the selvages themselves will do the work of side hems and can be hidden in the gathers. (The instructions that follow include sewing the lengths into panels and hemming the sides, in case the selvages are extra-wide or of a contrasting color.)

Almost any lightweight or medium-weight smoothly woven fabric — chintz, broadcloth, muslin — will shirr well. Avoid stiff cloth, such as canvas, and stretchy fabrics, such as jersey.

For generous gathers, a panel made of lightweight or medium-weight fabric should be two and a half times as wide as its rods are long. A thicker fabric's width should be twice the rod length, and a panel of very sheer fabric three times as wide as the rods are long.

Figure the total yardage needed after drawing a plan of each wall, similar to the one at top, opposite, to determine where the rods will be installed. To calculate the amount of fabric needed for each pair of one upper and one lower rod, first multiply the rod length by 2, 2½ or 3, depending on the fabric, as noted above. Then divide by the fabric width. The result is the number of side-by-side pieces of fabric needed to fit that pair of rods. When the result includes a fraction, round it up to the next whole number if the fraction is half or more, down if the fraction is less

than half. If the rod length is less than one third the fabric width, cut the fabric lengthwise and hem the edge *(Step 4)*.

To determine the length of each piece, start with the distance from the upper rod to the lower rod, and add 4 inches for the distance the 2-inch headings will extend beyond the rods. Next, add 16 inches for folds involved in making the casings and headings, and another 2 inches to ensure that the panel will reach from rod to rod without being stretched. The result is the cut length — the actual length of the pieces that will be used to make the panel. If the fabric has a pattern that requires matching where piece meets piece, add the length of one pattern repeat. (It is not economical to buy patterned fabric with a repeat longer than about 10 inches.)

Multiply the cut length by the number of pieces needed for the pair of rods, and then divide by 36 to get the yardage. Figure the yardage for each pair of rods and add the results together, along with a 10 per cent allowance for mistakes in measuring or cutting.

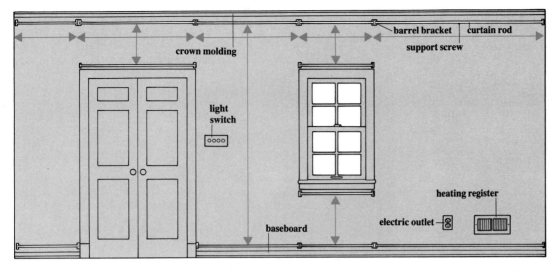

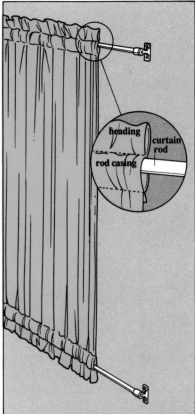

Anatomy of a shirred-fabric wall. Drawing a diagram for each wall, similar to the one above, will help you determine where to install curtain rods, as well as how much fabric to buy *(text, opposite)*. Include the dimensions (as indicated here by arrows) of each separate wall area that will require a pair of rods, and sketch in the placement of the rods. No rod should exceed 6 feet in length; the gathered fabric for longer rods would be too unwieldy. The diagram should also show the approximate positions of any electric outlets or switches and heating or cooling registers. Openings for these are cut in the fabric after the panels are installed *(Step 9)*.

Each pair of rods fits into casings sewed into the top and bottom of a fabric panel *(right)*. Headings on the panel cover the segments of wall that are directly above and below the rods.

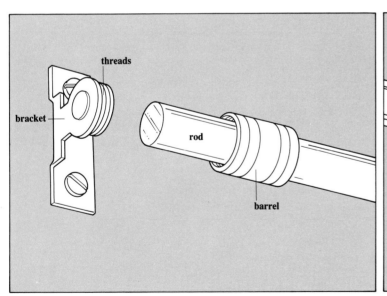

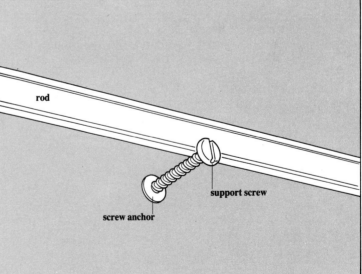

1 **Installing the curtain rods.** Install the ⅜-inch barrel brackets with screw anchors or other fasteners *(page 125)* before cutting the rods to length. Position the brackets ½ inch from corners and 1¾ inches from the ceiling, crown molding, baseboard, or top or bottom of window frames or doorframes. Adjacent brackets should nearly butt each other end to end. Measure the distance between each pair of mounted brackets, from outside end to outside end. Using bolt cutters or a hacksaw with a blade that has 32 teeth per inch, cut the steel rod ½ to ⅝ inch shorter than this measurement. Insert one end of the rod into one bracket. Remove the barrel from the other bracket and slip it over the opposite end of the rod *(above, left)*. Align the tip of the rod with the bracket threads, and screw the barrel onto the bracket, enclosing the tip of the rod. A rod longer than 4 feet should be supported by a screw near its center: Drill a pilot hole in the wall at the level of the rod, insert a screw anchor and drive a 2½-inch No. 8 round-head or pan-head screw into the anchor until its head protrudes only ⅛ to ¼ inch past the rod *(above, right)*. Then rest the rod on top of the screw. ▶

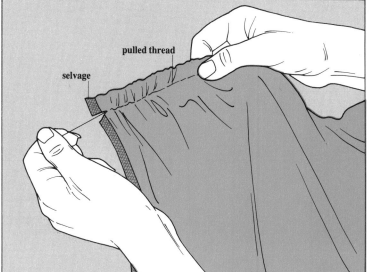

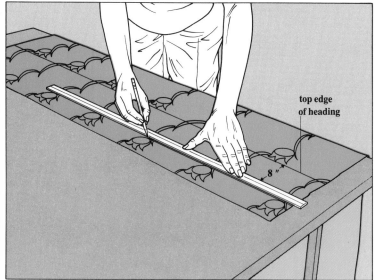

2 **Cutting the fabric straight.** If your fabric is a solid color, has a vertical stripe or is printed with a pattern so small that it is not necessary to match the design where pieces of fabric meet, clip through the selvage at one side, about an inch from the fabric's end. Then pick out the end of a crosswise thread and pull it gently, gathering the fabric along it with your fingers *(above, left)*. If the thread breaks, pick out the broken end with a pin and continue pulling. When you have pulled the thread all the way out, selvage to selvage, straighten the fabric and cut along the line left by the missing thread. Next, measure down the length needed to make the panel — the cut length, as it is called. Pull another thread and cut there.

This second cut can serve as the first cut for the next length of fabric.

To cut a print that must be matched, find the part of the repeating pattern you wish to align at the top heading; it must be at least 8 inches from the top end of the fabric. Lay a straightedge across this part of the design and mark a light chalk or pencil line; the line marks the heading's top edge. Draw a second line exactly 8 inches above the first line *(above, right)* and cut the fabric along it. From that cut, measure the cut length needed for the panel, align the straightedge and cut again. To cut the next length, find the same part of the pattern that you chose for the top heading of the first length, and mark and cut it at precisely the same places.

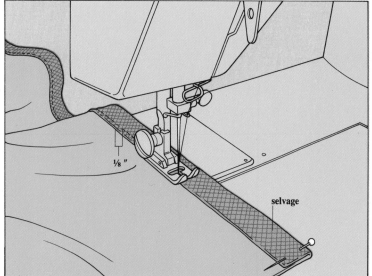

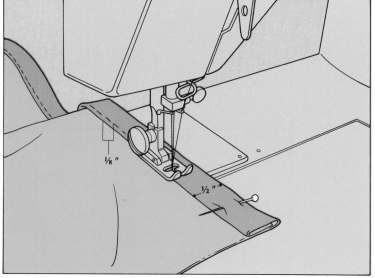

4 **Hemming panel edges.** Unobtrusive selvages along the sides of completed panels may be left unhemmed. But if the selvage is wide, or a different color from the fabric, you should hem it. Fold the selvage back and pin it. With the sewing machine still set at eight stitches per inch, stitch the selvage in place ⅛ inch from its edge *(above, left)*. A panel cut lengthwise to fit a very short curtain rod will have a raw edge that must be hemmed. Turn the fabric back along the cut edge in a ½-inch double fold, pin it in place and stitch ⅛ inch in from the edge of the hem *(above, right)*.

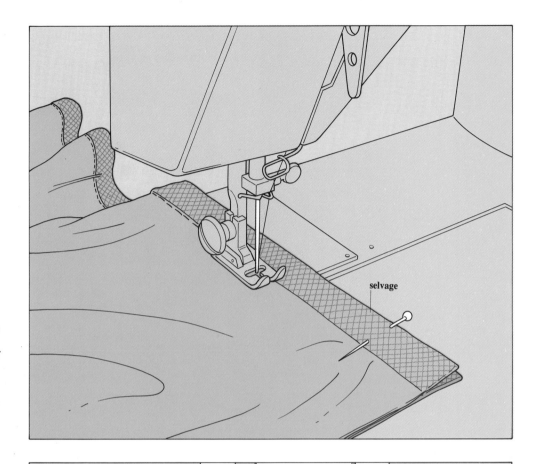

3 **Sewing lengths together.** Place two lengths of fabric face to face, aligning their top edges and the selvages along one side. Pin the selvages together. With your machine set for a straight, long stitch (eight stitches to the inch), sew along the inside edge of the selvage *(right)*, removing the pins as you go. Sew together the number of lengths of fabric needed to form the panel for one rod.

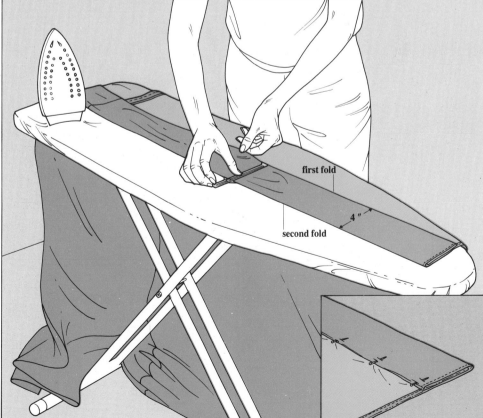

5 **Folding down the casing.** Place the top segment of the panel face down and lengthwise on an ironing board. Starting at one side, fold the top of the panel down 4 inches, pressing the fold as you go (press any seams to one side). When you reach the other side, work your way back, folding the top down another 4 inches *(right)*, pressing the second fold and pinning along the first fold *(inset).* ▶

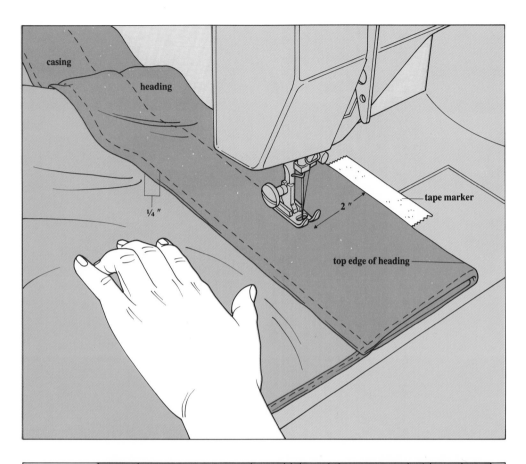

6 **Sewing the casing.** Stitch across the panel ¼ inch from the pinned fold, removing the pins as you go. Then stick a strip of tape on the sewing-machine base 2 inches to the right of the needle. Using the tape as a guide, stitch a seam 2 inches from the top edge of the heading *(left)* to form a casing and heading. Repeat Step 5 and this step to create the bottom casing and heading.

8 **Securing the panel bottom.** Gather the casing on the bottom rod and install the rod in the brackets the same way you did the top rod. Evenly distribute the gathers and tug the heading downward to straighten the folds and ease the tension on the bottom rod. If the panel is so tight that it causes either rod to bow, take it down, remove the lower-casing stitches with a seam ripper and follow Steps 5 and 6 to remake the casing and heading, but with 3½-inch instead of 4-inch folds. Then adjust the measurements for the rest of the panels accordingly.

7 **Hanging the panel.** Slide the top curtain rod into the top casing, gathering the fabric evenly and straightening the heading as you go. Slip one end of the rod into its bracket. Attach the other end of the rod to the second bracket as described in Step 1. After adjusting the gathers and heading, hook the rod and fabric over any support screws.

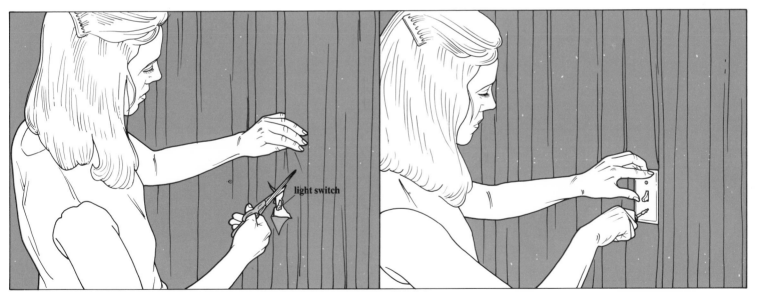

9 **Cutting fixture openings.** After all the panels are installed and the folds arranged, feel behind the fabric for each light switch or electric outlet, referring to your wall diagram for guidance. Cut a small X in the fabric in front of the switch plate or outlet cover *(above, left)*, making sure that the ends of the X are 1 inch short of each corner of the plate or cover. Cut off the excess triangles of fabric. Unscrew the plate and reinstall it over the cut edges of the fabric *(above, right)*, adjusting the gathers around the plate and making sure no fabric is dangerously close to the wiring connections inside the switch or outlet box. At a heating register, cut an X in the fabric, unscrew the register at each corner and reinstall it over the fabric, screwing through the fabric edges if necessary.

Easy elegance: Fabric stapled to the wall

Fabric-covered walls look extravagant, but they can be remarkably inexpensive and easy to create. Low-cost fabrics, uncut except for length, just need to be fitted to a wall and stapled side by side. The effect is similar to wallpaper, but fabrics have no need for messy adhesives and painstaking wall preparation. Stapled fabric can cover unsightly or damaged walls; if the walls are dark enough to show through the fabric, they can be lightened with a coat of paint.

Fabric offers textures, designs and widths not available in paper: Even bedsheets and bedspreads are candidates for covering walls. However, lightweight but tightly woven — even stiff — cotton blends are the simplest fabrics to work with, and a small to medium pattern with a frequent repeat is more economical for matching seams.

Though fabric walls seem exotic, the only maintenance they need is an occasional vacuuming. At any time, the fabric is readily removable — for cleaning and reuse, if you like. A coat of paint will fill leftover staple holes if you tire of the fabric treatment.

Where the fabric panels are stapled side by side, a special technique called backtacking hides the staples within an unobtrusive double seam. A tack strip — a narrow cardboard strip sold in rolls by upholstery shops — is positioned on top of the adjacent fabric edges, and staples are driven through fabric and tack strip simultaneously. The tack strip invisibly reinforces the seam and keeps it straight.

A spring-powered manual staple gun will drive staples into the hardest plaster. Choose a gun that ejects the staples flush with the head of the tool, so you can staple into corners.

To position the first panel vertically, a plumb chalk line is snapped on the wall just to the right of the first corner, and the fabric edge is aligned with it. Plumb lines are also snapped on the edges of succeeding panels to determine the tack-strip positions. Panels are installed right over windows, door and outlets; holes are cut for them last. The raw edges around these openings, and along the ceiling and baseboard, are finished with ribbon braid or other fabric trim.

To determine the number of yards of fabric to buy, add the widths of the walls to be covered — measured in inches — and divide this sum by the fabric width; round up to the next whole number to find the number of panels of fabric needed. Measure the wall height in inches from ceiling line or molding to floor or baseboard, and add 4 inches — providing 2 inches for trimming at the top and bottom of each panel.

If the fabric is patterned, add to the wall height the length of the pattern repeat — the distance from where a complete design starts to where it begins to repeat. Divide the sum by 36 and multiply this figure by the number of panels; round up the result again to calculate the number of yards needed. Purchase 10 per cent more than this amount to allow for waste. The length of tack strip to buy equals the number of panels times the height of the wall, plus a few yards extra for cutting errors.

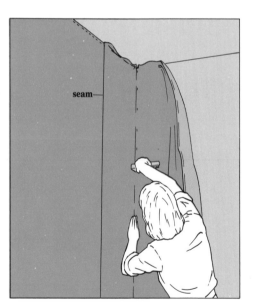

 Forming a midwall seam. Pin the second panel wrong side out over the first. Align the panels along their right edges, match the pattern there and push in a few pins. Snap a vertical chalk line on the top panel just left of the selvage. Align the left edge of the tack strip with the chalk line; be sure the strip covers the left sides of both selvages. Staple the tack strip every 6 inches, then every inch, removing the pushpins as you go. Fold the panel to the right, pin and staple it as in Step 2.

4 Stapling a corner panel. Pull the last panel toward an inside corner. Staple it to the adjoining wall near the top corner; then drive in staples every 6 inches, pulling the panel taut. Neatly cut off excess fabric 1 inch outside the staples. If the fabric has no pattern, follow Steps 1 and 2 to round the corner. For an outside corner, round it and staple the fabric 3 or 4 inches past it. Cut off the excess 1 inch beyond the staples. Hang the next panel *(Step 3)*.

5 Matching the pattern in a corner. Hang a panel wrong side out over the previous panel, its right selvage extended several inches beyond the corner. Fold the selvage back at the corner, exposing the fabric's print. Match a pattern element with the same pattern element on the panel behind it and drive a staple there. Match the pattern in several more places along the corner. Follow Steps 1 and 2 to install the panel, but do not snap a chalk line.

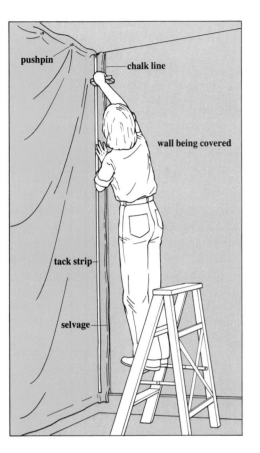

pushpin

chalk line

wall being covered

tack strip

selvage

1 **Stapling the first corner panel.** Cut the first fabric strip to fit the height of the wall plus 4 inches for trimming and, if needed, extra length for matching the pattern as explained in Step 2, page 74. Snap a vertical chalk line on the wall 1 or 2 inches to the right of the corner. With pushpins, loosely hang the fabric wrong side out on the adjoining wall, letting the right selvage slightly overlap the plumb line, and leaving 2 inches at top and bottom. Push the left edge of a tack strip into the corner on top of the fabric and staple it to the wall from top to bottom every 6 inches; keep the selvage edge aligned with the plumb line. Fill in the spaces by driving staples 1 inch apart.

2 **Pulling panel to the right.** Remove the pushpins, and fold the panel over the tack strip and onto the right wall. Repin the panel across the top, this time pulling the fabric taut. Starting at the upper right corner, staple through the selvage into the wall every 6 inches, smoothing the fabric taut to the right before driving each staple. Remove the pushpins, and staple the panel ¼ inch from the ceiling and the baseboard, first every 6 inches, then every inch. Trim away excess fabric with a sharp utility knife, leaving only a ¼-inch allowance.

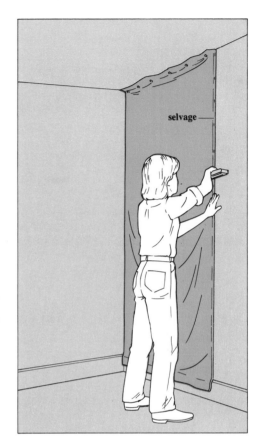

selvage

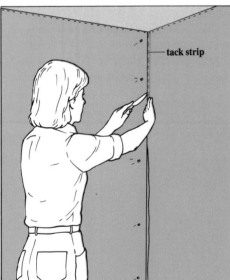

tack strip

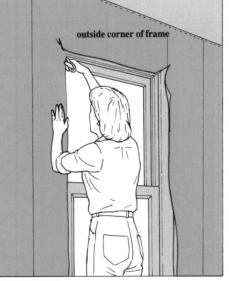

outside corner of frame

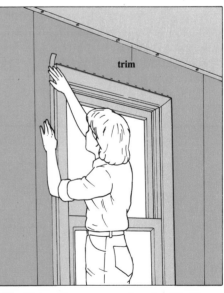

trim

6 **Finishing the final panel edge.** Pull the last panel toward the corner and pin it along the corner to hold it taut. Staple the panel along the ceiling and baseboard, and trim it. Neatly cut excess fabric from the right edge ¼ to ½ inch beyond the corner. Turn the edge back and run a bead of white glue along the corner. Tuck the edge under the tack strip of the adjoining panel, using a table knife or letter opener. Remove the pins after 1 hour.

7 **Cutting around a window or door.** Cut away the fabric within the window frame or doorframe. At each corner, make a diagonal cut extending to, but not beyond, the outside corner of the frame *(above)*. Staple the fabric to the wall all around the opening, ⅛ to ¼ inch from the frame edge, setting the staples 1 inch apart. Trim the fabric edges with a utility knife. To cut an opening for an electric outlet, follow Step 9, page 77.

8 **Gluing trim over exposed staples.** Working 1 foot at a time, spread white glue sparingly along the line of staples at the ceiling and baseboard, and around window frames and doorframes. Press ribbon or braid on the glue; cut the ends to fit with scissors before pressing them down — and apply a little extra glue to prevent raveling. Hold the trim in place with pushpins until the glue dries — about ½ hour.

Wood:
Warm and traditional

Handsome appearance, and the considerable cost that once went with its installation, made wood paneling a hallmark of fine homes for generations — testament to both the homeowner's prosperity and the carpenter's skill. Today, thanks to mass production of lumber and the development of new wood products, the effect of paneled walls is within almost everyone's budget and carpentry ability.

The simplest way to achieve a classic look is to embellish the walls with wood molding. Once carved by skilled craftsmen, decorative moldings are now milled by machine and are readily available in a plethora of styles. Used as trim, they can dignify the plainest walls and evoke traditional paneling motifs *(page 94)*. Similar effects can be achieved by painting stripes that simulate molding, fooling the eye as *trompe l'oeil* designs *(pages 95-99)*.

For completely lining a wall with wood, there are two basic alternatives. The older, more traditional method is to use solid boards, like those shown on pages 82-83. The boards are applied to the wall, one at a time, in vertical, horizontal or even diagonal strips. The newer, more widely employed form of paneling is 4-by-8-foot — and, when ordered specially, 4-by-10-foot — sheets that are attached directly to walls with adhesive *(pages 108-112)*. As indicat-ed in the chart at right, there are four basic sheet-paneling choices: plywood veneered with real wood, and plywood, hardboard or particleboard laminated with patterned paper or printed with wood-grain patterns. The photographs below are samples of wood-veneer plywood.

The plywood consists of three layers of wood glued together. The grains of adjacent layers run at right angles to each other, which strengthens the sheets and helps counteract the wood's natural tendency to shrink or swell with changes in temperature and humidity. Plywood wall paneling typically is made of two wood species. The core is often an inexpensive tropical hardwood, such as luaun, or Philippine mahogany, from a fast-growing tree with relatively little grain to harbor moisture. This makes the core resist changes in humidity and gives the panel added stability.

The sheets are veneered with more vividly patterned and thus innately more attractive woods such as birch, oak or pine. The wood is most commonly processed by a technique called rotary cutting, in which thin sheets of veneer are unfurled from a log, like paper from a roll. The veneer retains all of the knots, wormholes, bird pecks and idiosyncratic grain patterns that were present in the tree itself.

Manufacturers may leave these natural effects intact, simply staining the wood, then coating it with a clear fin-

Cedar, dark stain   Oak, light stain   Birch, dark stain, embossed   Ponderosa pine, gray stain   Birch, medium stain,

ish. Or they may enhance the wood's characteristics by embossing its surface, raising its grain with wire brushes, or printing on additional grain patterns. Thus, the five samples of birch paneling below look considerably different from one another. Each has been stained a different color, and two have had additional surface treatment. The third panel from the left is embossed with marks that mimic the random nicks of age. The fifth panel from the left has been run through a giant printing press that applied extra grain patterns to accentuate the natural grain of the veneer.

A similar process is used to print simulated grain directly on the surface of hardboard, particleboard and plywood faced with inexpensive veneers. The panels are first coat-ed with an opaque color, then printed with photographical-ly reproduced wood grains. Even more common are panels covered with grain-patterned paper. The paper is glued to the panels, then protected with a transparent coating.

Most wall-panel sheets are incised with shallow parallel grooves — simulated joints that make the sheets appear to be assembled from boards. You may, however, order more formal-looking ungrooved panels of real-wood veneer like that on page 108. A lumber dealer can also obtain sheets veneered with rare and exotic woods, such as rosewood or teak. These generally have unfinished surfaces, and must be stained and finished by hand after they have been installed.

Basic Offerings in Sheet Paneling

Form	Composition	Advantages	Limitations
Wood veneer on plywood	Real-wood veneer over plywood. Commonly available softwood veneers include California redwood, knotty pine and red cedar; popular hardwoods include oak, walnut and birch. Veneer generally protected by clear finish. Veneer usually $\frac{1}{32}$ inch thick, panel $\frac{1}{4}$ inch thick.	Appearance of solid wood at much less cost. Prefinished. Excellent resistance to moisture, sound and impact. Each panel unique in appearance. Some expensive veneers such as teak, rosewood and mahogany available.	Moderately expensive. Splinters easily.
Simulated wood pattern on plywood	Plywood printed with wood-grain patterns or laminated with paper. Panels $\frac{5}{32}$ or $\frac{3}{16}$ inch thick.	Prefinished. Economical. Strong and flexible. Easily bent to fit curved walls.	Splinters easily.
Simulated wood pattern on hardboard	Heated and compressed wood fibers printed with wood-grain patterns or laminated with paper. Panels $\frac{5}{32}$ or $\frac{3}{16}$ inch thick.	Prefinished. Economical. Great variety of colors and grain patterns. Moderately strong.	Dulls saw blades quickly.
Simulated wood pattern on particleboard	Compressed and glued wood particles or chips printed with wood-grain patterns or laminated with printed paper. Panels $\frac{3}{16}$ inch thick.	Inexpensive.	Weak, rigid and brittle Does not hold nails well. Dulls saw blades quickly.

Ponderosa pine, white stain   Birch, medium stain   Birch, light stain   Blue pine, medium stain, embossed   Birch, light stain

A choice of boards for enhancing walls

For solid wood paneling, boards come in two types of configuration: square-edged and mill-edged. Square-edged boards are the standard dimensional lumber used for any carpentry chore; mill-edged boards are carved by machine to interlock with one another, and many styles are specially produced for paneling. Except for porch ceiling boards *(far right, top)*, all of the boards are sized before smoothing and thus are nominally 1 inch, but actually ¾ inch, thick. Similarly, their nominal widths of 2 to 12 inches represent actual widths of 1½ to 11¼ inches.

Because the boards will expand and contract with changes in temperature and humidity, they cannot be glued to walls as most sheet paneling is. Instead, they are nailed directly to the studs or to a framework of 1-by-3 furring strips *(page 113)*. In general, the panels look best when combined with baseboard and ceiling moldings that, like the samples shown here, conceal the inevitable small irregularities at top and bottom.

Straight-edged boards are customarily arranged in overlapping configurations to produce casual, three-dimensional effects such as those below. They are rarely butted edge-to-edge against their neighbors because the wood's normal expansion and contraction would create gaps between the boards.

Mill-edged boards are shaped to create two types of joints — tongue-and-groove and shiplap. Neat, able to expand and contract without showing gaps, these boards can be installed diagonally as well as horizontally or vertically.

Both straight- and mill-edged boards can be found in a full range of softwoods, such as pine, cedar, redwood, fir and spruce, and in hardwoods such as birch, cherry, maple, oak and walnut. The supply and expense of different species vary according to geographic location. For the most part, solid wood boards are available only as unfinished lumber and must be finished after they have been installed.

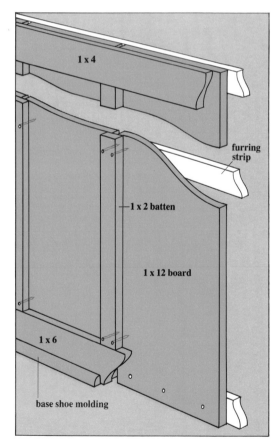

Square-Edged

Among the most popular patterns of paneling created with conventionally milled, straight-edged lumber are the two shown here. The traditional board-and-batten design *(left)* consists of wide boards, set ½ inch apart, with narrow battens nailed over the gaps. The boards here are 1-by-12s; the battens are 1-by-2s. The baseboard is made of 1-by-6s with base shoe molding. Like the 1-by-4s at the ceiling, the 1-by-6s run across the faces of the boards, flush with the ends of the battens.

Board-on-board paneling *(right)* creates channels between boards. In the example here, 1-by-4s spaced 4 inches apart are covered by 1-by-6s spaced 2 inches apart. The base and ceiling moldings are 1-by-4s and 1-by-3s respectively.

For each of these installations — and for any alternate ones using different-size lumber or different spacing — the first layer of boards is nailed in place with eightpenny nails driven through the top and bottom furring strips and into the wall behind. The baseboard and ceiling moldings are then fastened to the face of the boards with sixpenny finishing nails. Finally, the battens or top boards are trimmed to fit, then nailed just above the baseboard, below the ceiling molding and at the furring strips in between, with sixpenny finishing nails.

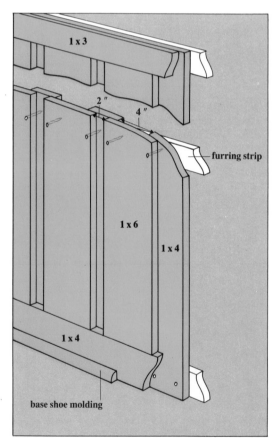

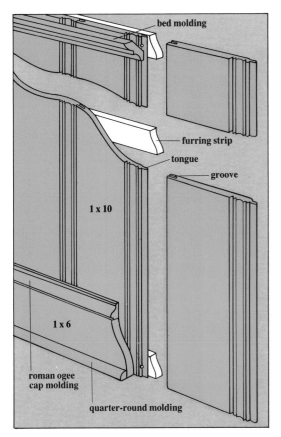

Tongue-and-Groove

In tongue-and-groove paneling, the protruding tongue along the edge of one board fits into a groove channeled in the opposite edge of an adjoining board. Each board is nailed to furring strips through the base of the tongue, a technique called blind nailing because the nailheads are hidden by the groove of the next board.

The example at left shows one way tongue-and-groove boards can be carved and beaded to achieve various decorative effects. These are 1-by-10s; a strip of quarter-round and a 1-by-6 baseboard topped by roman ogee cap molding finish their base; they are topped by bed molding.

The boards at right, and in the photograph on page 114, are 4-inch-wide porch ceiling boards, which are thinner than average tongue-and-groove boards — 5/16 inch rather than 3/4 inch thick — and thus take up slightly less room when installed over an existing wall. These are grooved down the center to create the illusion of 2-inch-wide strips. This saves installation time by cutting in half the number of boards that would otherwise be needed to achieve the same effect. These boards are trimmed with base shoe molding, 1-by-4 baseboard and ogee cap molding at the floor, and cove molding at the ceiling.

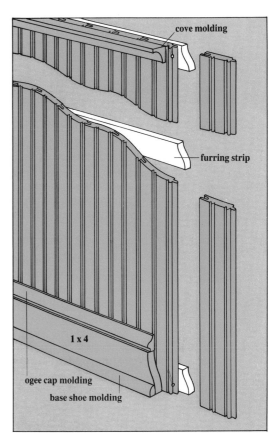

Shiplap

Overlapping shiplap joints, like interlocking tongue-and-groove joints, produce seams that can expand and contract without creating gaps. Shiplap boards are somewhat easier to install because they do not require precision blind nailing. They are face-nailed to the furring strips behind them. The nailheads are then recessed with a nail set and filled with putty.

Like tongue-and-groove boards, shiplap boards come in a variety of styles and sizes. The 1-by-6s at left — with 4-inch ranch base molding and 3-inch clamshell ceiling molding — have rounded edges that fit together to impart a smooth, slightly undulating look to the wall. The random-width boards at right — ranging in size from 1-by-3 to 1-by-8 — have rough-textured faces to simulate the appearance of rustic, weathered barn siding. The 4-inch baseboard and the 3-inch ceiling molding are the same type of shiplap boards ripped (cut along the grain) to create narrow strips.

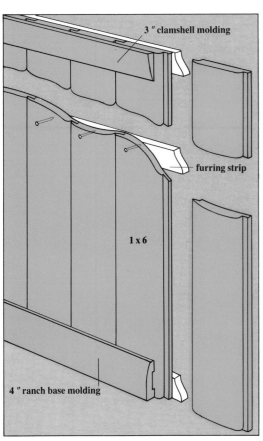

Putting the best face on wood walls

With the exception of factory-finished paneling, wood-clad walls require finishing like fine wood furniture. Typically, wood is first stained to enhance or alter its natural color; then it is coated with a clear finish to protect its surface. Many woods are also treated with a sealer.

On softwoods, which tend to absorb stain unevenly, a sealer applied directly to the raw wood controls stain penetration. Sealers also prevent softwood resins from bleeding into stains and finishes. On both hardwoods and softwoods, a sealer may be used over the stain to provide a base for the finish coat and a smoother appearance. As the chart below indicates, the type of sealer used depends on whether it will be applied before or after staining, and on the type of stain or finish that will be applied over it.

Stains range from almost transparent dye types to pigmented, semiopaque coatings. Most stains used on walls are oil-based and are divided into two categories: penetrating and nonpenetrating. Penetrating stains contain transparent dyes that soak deeply into the wood, accentuating its grain. Nonpenetrating stains are semiopaque, and contain pigments that downplay the grain and produce a more uniform appearance.

Varnishes and clear penetrating oils are finishes — final-stage coatings that protect the wood, while imparting sheen to its surface. Penetrating oils, the traditional finish employed on wood walls, produce a soft luster; varnishes produce a tough film.

The charts here provide general guidelines for comparison in each of the three categories. However, the formulas of various manufacturers differ, affecting how a product is applied, how long it takes to dry, and what its compatibility with other materials may be. Before you settle on a finishing strategy, try the entire sequence of sealer, stain and finish on a sample board to see that it produces the results you want. Be sure, also, to follow the manufacturer's instructions. If in doubt, consult a knowledgeable dealer.

Sealers to Prime and Shield

Purpose	Stain/finish to follow	Sealer to use
Beneath stains: To reduce stain penetration (principally in softwoods). To keep natural resins of softwoods from bleeding into stain.	Oil-based stains, penetrating and nonpenetrating	1 part boiled linseed oil to 1 part mineral spirits
	Solvent-based stains, including alcohol and non-grain-raising (NGR) stains	8 parts denatured alcohol to 1 part shellac
Over stains: To prevent stain from bleeding into finish. To prepare surface for fine sanding. On softwoods not sealed prior to staining, to keep resins from bleeding into finish.	Polyurethane varnish	1 part polyurethane varnish to 1 part mineral spirits
	Varnishes other than polyurethane	8 parts denatured alcohol to 1 part shellac; or same varnish as finish — 1 part varnish to 1 part mineral spirits
	Penetrating oil finish	No sealer required between stain and oil finish

Stains — Solutions That Accentuate Wood Grain

Type	Ingredients	Uses	Advantages	Limitations
Penetrating oil	Aniline dyes dissolved in oil and oleoresins	For all woods.	Soaks deeply to dye wood fibers. Easy to use.	Dries slowly: 12-24 hours. May overemphasize grain, producing striped appearance.
Nonpenetrating oil	Pigment dissolved in oil and oleoresins	For woods with little graining. To match unmatched woods.	Coats wood fibers like thin paint. Easy to control.	Dries slowly: 12-24 hours. May obscure grain entirely if applied in a thick coat. Pigment will settle out of suspension to produce uneven results unless stirred frequently. Colors are muted. Does not cover well on hardwood.
Alcohol-based NGR (non-grain-raising) stains	Powdered dyes dissolved in denatured alcohol or other fast-evaporating solvents	For woods with beautiful grain.	Transparent. Penetrates deeply. Can be intermixed to make custom stains. Does not raise grain. Fast-drying.	Difficult to apply and control; overlaps show up as dark streaks. Produces flammable, potentially harmful vapors; use only in well-ventilated areas.
Water-based	Powdered dyes dissolved in water	For woods with beautiful grain.	Fast-drying. Excellent color qualities. Penetrates deeply.	Raises grain, so wood requires extra sanding. Tends to cause swelling and warping. Difficult to mix colors for predictable results.
Double-duty stains	Mix of stain and varnish	For all woods.	One-step application saves time.	Somewhat more expensive than stain and varnish bought separately. Limited range of colors. Does not provide a high-quality finish; color is in top coat — not on the wood. When scratched or chipped, bare, unstained wood shows.

Finishes: Coatings That Protect and Polish

Type	Ingredients	Characteristics	Advantages	Limitations
Acrylic varnish	Acrylic resins dissolved in fast-evaporating solvents	Produces hard film of crystal clarity, with no hint of amber tint. Available in flat, semigloss and high-gloss lusters.	Allows true color of wood to show through. Does not yellow with age or exposure to sun. Dries quickly.	Because it dries quickly, may be difficult to apply unless sprayed on. Only moderately resistant to wear. Solvents produce flammable vapors.
Alkyd varnish	Alkyd resins, vegetable oils, solvents and driers	Produces hard, transparent film. Available in high-gloss and semigloss lusters.	Easy to apply with predictably good results.	Darkens wood slightly. Solvents produce flammable vapors.
Penetrating oil	Boiled linseed oil, heat-treated tung oil or other vegetable oil	Produces lustrous oil finish. Frequent applications create a thin film.	Inexpensive. Easy to apply.	Darkens wood considerably. May take two days to dry between coats. Needs waxing for durability. Linseed oil requires considerable rubbing to produce glowing finish.
Polyurethane varnish	Polyurethane (urethane) resins combined with oils, solvents and driers	Produces a hard, transparent film. Flat, semigloss and high-gloss lusters.	Extremely tough. Fairly water-resistant.	Darkens with age., Solvents produce flammable, potentially harmful vapors.

Installing Baseboard with Cap and Shoe Moldings

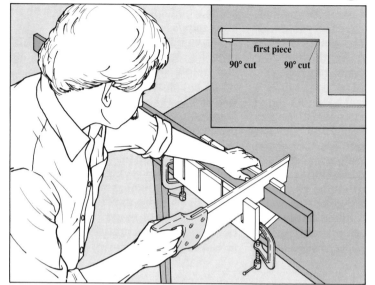

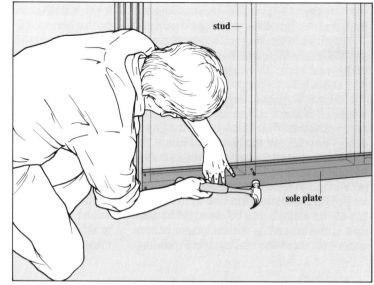

1 **Cutting the first board.** Measure from the doorframe to the first corner, here an inside corner *(inset)*. Mark that length on top of a piece of baseboard molding. (Here, dressed 1-by-4 lumber, surfaced smooth on four sides, is used instead of curved-profile baseboard molding; cap and shoe molding will be added to it after it is installed.) Hold the baseboard to the back of the miter box and align each of the end marks in turn with the 90° slots. Insert a backsaw in the slots, lowering it into the board with smooth, steady strokes. Cut all the way to the bottom of the miter box. (If your first board ends at an outside corner, see Step 3.)

2 **Fastening the first board.** Locate and mark the positions of wall studs *(page 19)* between the door and the first corner. Starting at the door end, fasten the cut baseboard flat against the wall with sixpenny finishing nails driven into the studs and the sole plate. Drive two nails ¾ inch from the doorframe: one ¾ inch up from the floor and the other ¾ inch down from the top of the board. Drive pairs of nails at those heights into the wall studs and the sole plate along the length of the baseboard.

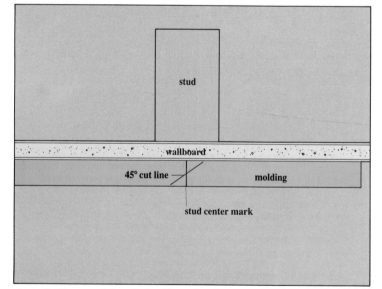

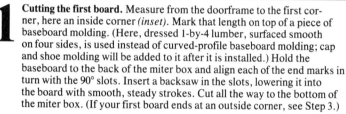

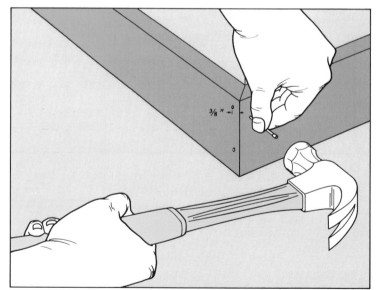

5 **Cutting an end for splicing.** Place the piece cut in Step 4 in position against the wall. On it mark the center of the farthest stud that the piece covers. Cut the board using the 45° slots running from left to right so that the cut bisects the stud center mark. This second cut, parallel to the first or corner cut, will be spliced to the next board in Step 8.

6 **Fastening the outside corner boards.** Hold the two boards that meet at the outside corner in place. If they meet in a snug joint, fasten them to the walls with sixpenny finishing nails driven into the studs and sole plate as in Step 2: Start nailing at the inside corner, as close as possible to the board installed in Step 2. Lock-nail the outside corner joint by driving two fourpenny finishing nails through each board into the end of the other board *(above)*.

    If a gap appears in the joint when the boards are first fitted into place, see Step 7 before fastening them to the walls.

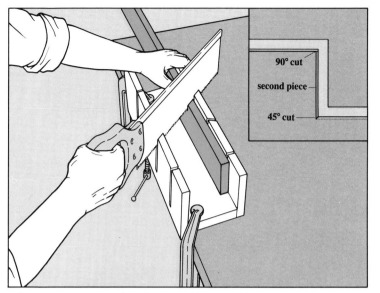

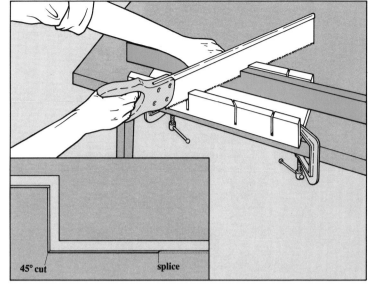

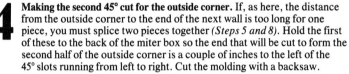

3 **Making the first 45° cut for an outside corner.** If you are using baseboard with a plain rectangular profile, as here, butt the square-cut end of a second piece into the inside corner against the piece already nailed to the wall. At the other end of the second piece, mark the back edge of the top where the board crosses the outside corner. Hold the board to the back of the miter box with the mark just to the left of a 45° slot that runs from right to left. Saw the board *(above)*, and hold it in place *(inset)* to check its length, but do not nail it to the wall until you have cut the board that completes the corner *(Steps 4-6)*.

If two pieces of molding with a curved profile meet at an inside corner, cope the end of the second one to fit the face of the first *(Steps 10-11)*.

4 **Making the second 45° cut for the outside corner.** If, as here, the distance from the outside corner to the end of the next wall is too long for one piece, you must splice two pieces together *(Steps 5 and 8)*. Hold the first of these to the back of the miter box so the end that will be cut to form the second half of the outside corner is a couple of inches to the left of the 45° slots running from left to right. Cut the molding with a backsaw.

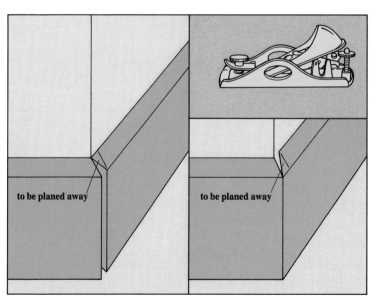

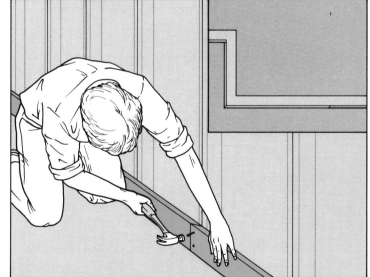

7 **Eliminating a gap at an outside corner.** If there is a gap in the corner joint when the boards are held in place *(Step 6)*, measure across it with a ruler. For a front gap that is up to ¼ inch wide, measure from the top of the back corner of one board a distance equal to the gap's width, make a mark and draw a line from the mark to the front corner *(above, left)*; divide a larger gap between both boards. For a back gap *(above, right)*, measure from the front corner. Then, using a sharp block plane *(inset)*, shave the wood to the line so the boards fit tightly.

If the front of the joint is snug, you may fill a back gap instead of planing the boards. Do it after all baseboard is installed. Use spackling compound as a filler if the molding will be painted, wood filler if it will be stained.

8 **Splicing boards together.** For the splice end of the board that will extend the molding along the long wall *(inset)*, make a 45° cut that is complementary to the splice cut at the end of the already-installed board. Cut the other end of the new board as required. Run a bead of carpenter's glue along the cut end of the installed board and press the matching end of the new board against it. Fasten the new board to studs along the wall with sixpenny finishing nails. Drive two of the nails through the overlapped sections into the stud and sole plate behind the splice. Using a damp rag, wipe off any excess glue. ▶

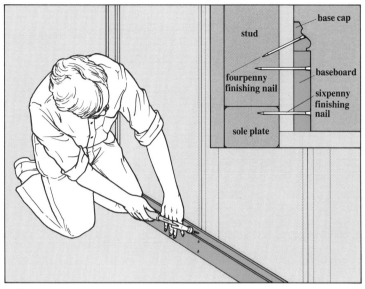

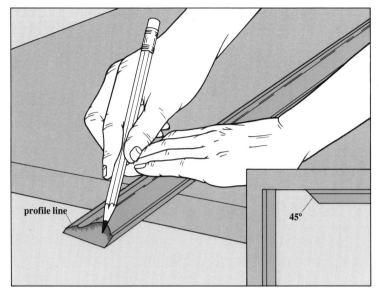

9 **Adding base cap molding.** To add base cap molding to the first board you installed, start by sawing a piece of the molding to the length of the board, making straight 90° cuts at both ends, just as you did for the baseboard *(Step 1)*. Place the molding in position atop the baseboard, and fasten it to the studs with fourpenny finishing nails. Drive the nails through a moderately thick section of the molding profile, if possible on a convex curve where the nail hole can be filled and sanded easily. Angle nails down through the wall and into the studs *(inset)* or, if the nail cannot reach the stud, into the top of the baseboard.

10 **Cutting cap molding.** Cut base cap molding for an outside corner or for a splice the same way that you cut the baseboard. But for an inside corner, you will need to shape the end of one molding piece with a coping saw so it will fit snugly onto the curved profile of the adjoining piece. Start by making a 45° cut on the inside-corner end of the piece that will be coped *(inset)*. The acute angle of the cut should point into the corner; therefore, for a piece to be installed on top of the second baseboard *(see page 89, Step 3, inset)*, make the cut in the right-to-left grooves of the miter box. Then mark the profile line along the curved, front edge of the cut by rubbing it with the side of a pencil lead *(above)*.

Installing Chair Rail

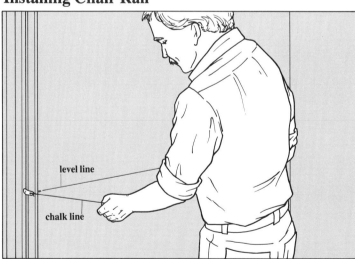

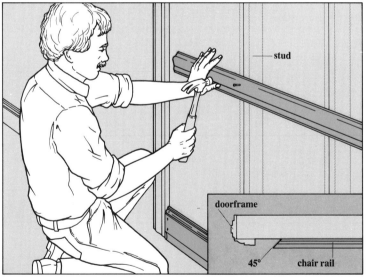

1 **Marking a line.** Alongside the doorframe and about 2 feet along the wall from the frame, mark the height for the top of the molding — usually 30 to 36 inches above the floor, or a third of the way up the wall. Using a carpenter's level as a straightedge, draw a line between the marks. With a helper if necessary, stretch a chalk line *(page 52)* from the doorframe to where the first length of chair rail will end (here, an inside corner), using the level line just drawn to make sure the string is level. Snap the string to leave a chalk impression along the length of the wall.

2 **Fashioning a chair-rail return.** Cut chair rail the same way you cut base cap molding, with one exception: If the rail is thicker than the door or window trim in its path, stop the molding 2 inches short of the casing by fashioning what is called a returned end, in which the profile of the chair rail turns a corner to cross the end of the molding. Start by cutting off the end of the molding at 45° with the acute angle at the molding's front — a left-to-right cut if dealing with the left end of a piece, as here *(inset)*, a right-to-left cut if putting a return on a right-hand end. The angled end will hold the return wedge, which you will cut in Step 3.

Attach the chair rail to the studs by aligning its top with the chalk line and driving finishing nails through a moderately thick portion *(above)*.

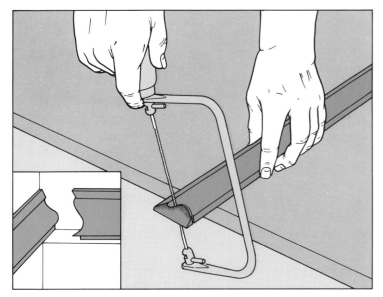

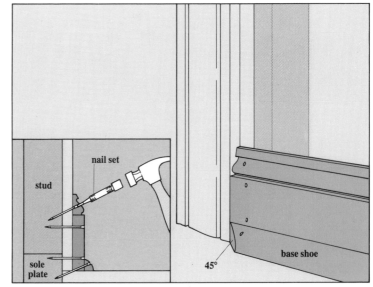

stud

nail set

sole plate

base shoe

45°

11 **Coping the profile.** Use a coping saw with a thin, fine-toothed (20 teeth to the inch) blade. Keeping the blade tilted slightly under the back of the molding as shown, cut along the pencil-marked edge. (To cope molding with a more complex profile, such as crown molding, tilt the blade much farther under the back of the piece.) Rotate the blade within the saw frame as necessary to keep the frame from striking the molding. The result should be a cut end that will butt snugly against the profile of the first piece *(inset)*.

Cut the other end of the molding as required — in this instance, mitered for an outer corner — before nailing the piece to the studs.

12 **Adding base shoe molding.** Cut base shoe molding just as you did the base cap molding, with one exception: Make a 45° cut angling toward the doorframe that the shoe molding abuts (here, a right-to-left cut). Fasten the molding with finishing nails driven through a moderately thick part of the profile. Remember to predrill holes if the molding is hardwood. Angle the nails so they reach through the baseboard into the sole plate or floor. Drive all visible nailheads below the surface with a hammer and a nail set *(inset)*. Cover the nailheads and fill gaps with spackling compound if the molding is to be painted and with tinted wood filler if it is to be stained. Sand with medium (100-grit) sandpaper, and paint or stain the molding.

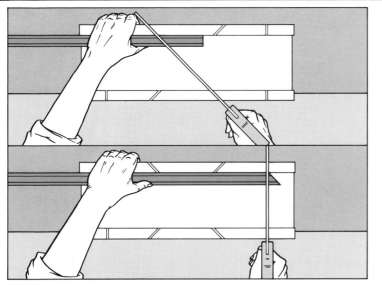

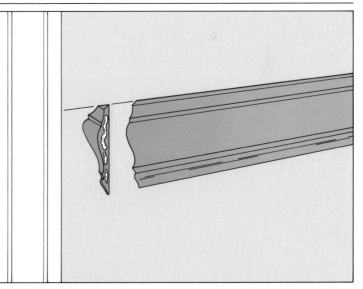

3 **Cutting the return wedge.** To make a return for the left end of a length of chair rail, hold a short scrap piece of the molding to the back of the miter box and make a 45° right-to-left cut on its right end *(top)*. (For a wedge to fit on a right-hand end, cut left to right near the left end.) Then, using the 90° slots, cut off the triangular wedge formed by the 45° cut *(bottom)*.

4 **Installing the return.** Apply carpenter's glue to the 45° cut edges of both the installed molding and the return wedge. Slide the wedge into the triangular gap between the installed molding and the wall, and press the glued surfaces together. Wipe off any excess glue with a damp cloth. Note: If the wedge does not fit tightly, use a 1/16-inch twist bit to drill a hole through the fattest part of its profile and fasten the wedge to the end of the molding with a No. 19 brad.

Installing Crown Molding

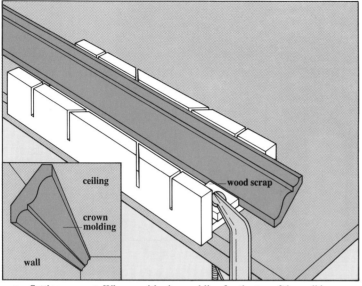

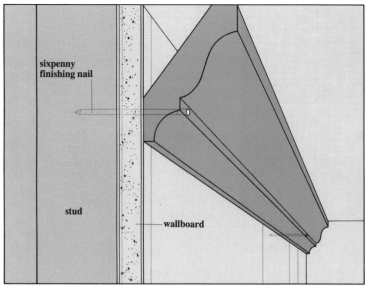

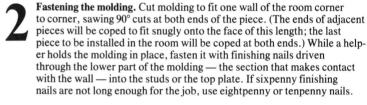

1 **Setting up a cut.** When positioning molding for the top of the wall in your miter box, think of the floor of the box as the ceiling and the back of the box as the wall. For example, to cut crown molding, which is installed as shown in the inset, position it in the box as seen above — upside down, with the part of the molding that will fit against the wall flat against the back of the box, and the part that will fit against the ceiling on the floor of the box. Note that this entails reversing the ends of the molding, so that a right-hand end on the wall will be on the left in the miter box. Place a narrow scrap of wood against the forward edge of the molding in the box, and clamp the scrap to the bottom of the box. It will hold the molding against the box's back wall.

2 **Fastening the molding.** Cut molding to fit one wall of the room corner to corner, sawing 90° cuts at both ends of the piece. (The ends of adjacent pieces will be coped to fit snugly onto the face of this length; the last piece to be installed in the room will be coped at both ends.) While a helper holds the molding in place, fasten it with finishing nails driven through the lower part of the molding — the section that makes contact with the wall — into the studs or the top plate. If sixpenny finishing nails are not long enough for the job, use eightpenny or tenpenny nails.

Installing Panel Molding

1 **Plotting the rectangles.** Measure the wall space from end to end and from bottom to top — here, chair rail to ceiling molding. Transfer these dimensions in scale to a piece of graph paper. Within the resulting lines, plot evenly spaced rectangles to represent the outside edges of the molding panels. Measuring up from the chair rail, put tick marks on the wall to indicate the outside of each corner of the rectangles. Then draw the vertical lines, using a carpenter's level to make them plumb (*above*). Finally, draw the horizontal lines.

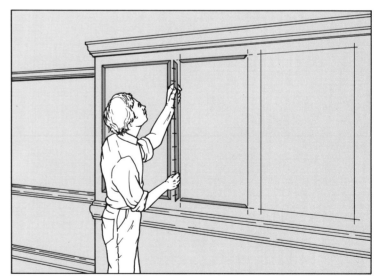

2 **Constructing a rectangle.** Hold a length of molding with its outside edge along the inside of one of the lines drawn for a rectangle. Mark the molding's outside edge where the rectangle's corners fall. Place the molding flat on the bottom of the miter box, outside edge against the back; make a 45° left-to-right cut for the right end and a 45° right-to-left cut for the left end. Remove the molding and start 1-inch brads into the middle, flat part of the profile 2 inches from each end and at 8-inch intervals — positioning the nails to go into studs wherever possible. Mark and cut the three other sides of a rectangle and start nails in them. Then put the top and bottom pieces in place and loosely fasten their end nails. Test the side pieces for fit and fasten all the pieces, adjusting the horizontal pieces if necessary.

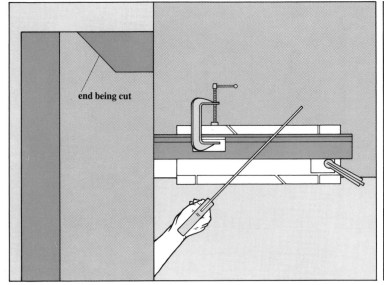

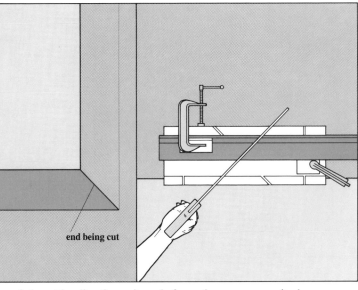

3 **Making angled cuts.** Because the molding is placed in the miter box upside down and reversed end for end *(Step 1)*, saw a 45° angle in the opposite direction from the alignment it will have after the molding is installed. For instance, to make the 45° right-to-left angle on a left-hand end that is to be coped for an inside corner *(above left, inset)*, cut the upside-down and reversed molding with the saw in the left-to-right slots *(above, left)*. For the right-to-left miter that makes a right-hand end fit an outside corner *(above right, inset)*, the sawing angle is again left to right. When in doubt about the cutting angle, remove the molding from the miter box, hold it in the position it will have when installed, and mark the cutting direction on its underface, where you can see it when you return the molding to the miter box upside down.

To cope crown molding *(page 91, Step 1)*, tilt the coping saw well under the back of the molding; for the most complicated profiles, tilt the saw as much as 45°. This technique, called undercutting, ensures a better fit, since it leaves only a thin front layer of wood that has to mate exactly with the profile of the adjacent piece of molding. If there are gaps in the resulting joint, shave the undercut edge to fit, using the coping saw, a utility knife or a wood file.

Built-Up Moldings for Ornate Effect

Simple molding profiles can be joined together to form more complex — and more visually interesting — combinations, such as the examples at right.

Baseboard *(pages 88-89)* offers the least room for play, the options being limited to a molded base — one with the cap built in — and shoe molding, or a rectangular base with added cap and shoe. But base elements can be used to splendid effect elsewhere. Base caps put bottom to bottom, for instance, form a symmetrical chair rail, while bed and base shoe molding combine with a dado-cut board to make a plate rail for displaying favorite dinnerware.

And diverse arrangements of base and cap — often in combination with cove or crown molding — look as handsome pointing down from the ceiling as up from the floor. But among cornices — built-up moldings at the top of the wall, like those near right — few compare with crown molding mounted on a molded base and trimmed with toothlike dentil molding. It confers on a room the classical look of a Greek temple.

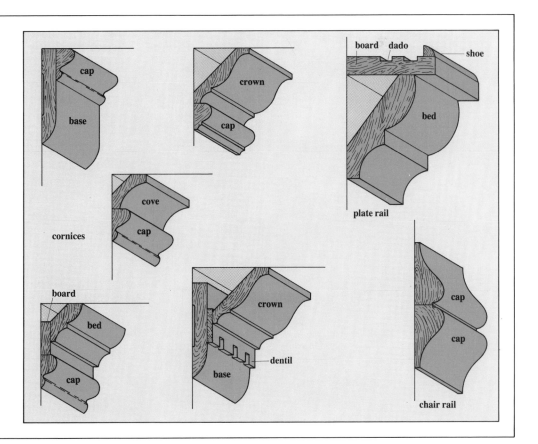

93

Designs with Molding

With a little imagination and some preliminary planning on graph paper, you can transform an unappealing, flat wall into your own creative masterpiece with wood molding. There is no need for special orders or fancy custom cuts. Stock molding, available at hardware stores and lumberyards, lends itself to limitless combinations; the patterns here illustrate but a sampling.

To design with wood molding, first assess the size and shape of the room and permanent wall elements such as doors, windows, a fireplace or built-in shelving. Make a plan of each wall to exact scale on graph paper. Then proportion a pattern to fit the overall space and adjust the pattern's arrangement to complement the room's permanent elements.

The molding can be painted to blend or contrast with existing furnishings, or stained to match or accent the natural wood grain of doors or walls. To obtain a perfect match with prefinished wall paneling or door units, you may prefer to buy prefinished molding.

Keep experimenting until you have the design you want. Then use the techniques demonstrated on the previous pages to cut and install molding pieces according to your design.

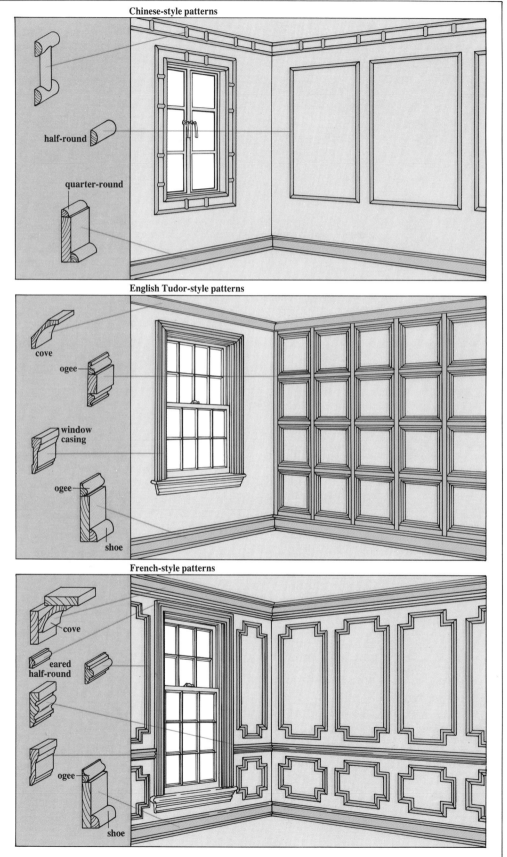

Mimicking molding with paint

Upon first glance, the walls below appear to be decorated with wood molding and paneling arranged to complement a classic frame-and-panel door. But only the baseboard is real trim; the ceiling molding, chair rail, wall panels and door panels are illusions, produced by paint, not wood.

To create this delightful *trompe l'oeil* (French for "trick of the eye"), you first mimic real wood trim with paint, then mimic the shadows that the room's lighting would produce around real trim.

Begin by making a scale drawing on graph paper of your walls and doors and the molding or paneling designs you want to create. (There are examples on the opposite page to inspire you.) Draw arrows showing the direction of the predominant light source. In the room below, the central ceiling light would create shadows below and to the right of real

molding on the left-hand wall and the door; it would create shadows below and to the left of real molding on the right-hand wall. In addition, the light would form shadows within the contours of real, ornamentally shaped molding.

Transferring the molding and paneling designs to the walls and doors requires snapping chalk lines at carefully measured locations. To facilitate cleanup, use chalk dust that matches the wall and door colors. Spread a dropcloth over the floor next to the wall where you are working, then — before you begin — snap the line over the cloth to rid it of excess chalk.

Drafting tape laid along the chalk lines will serve as guidelines for the painting and protect surfaces not to be painted. To prevent paint from seeping under the tape edges, seal tape borders by painting over them with the color already on the walls and door *(page 97, Step 3)*. Professionals

call this critical process "bedding the tape." You then paint between the bedded tapes, using a semigloss alkyd enamel that matches existing wood trim.

After the main trim color has dried, mix both light and dark shading tints out of artist's oil paints and equal amounts of the trim color and mineral spirits *(box, page 96)*, and paint the shadows.

Three types of brushes are called for: a ¼-inch artist's sable-bristle brush for bedding the tape; a 2-inch China-bristle trim brush for creating the trim; a ½-inch sable-bristle brush for shading. You will also need a palette knife for mixing shadow colors.

Although the work takes only a few hours at each stage, every paint coat must dry before you can apply another. After the painting is done, remove any chalk marks with a cloth dampened in a solution of warm water and a mild detergent.

Mixing the Shading Colors

Two shading colors — one pale and one dark — are enough. To paint panel molding, a chair rail and ceiling molding in a room about 10 by 12 feet, make up about 10 ounces of each color. Both have similar ingredients and are made the same way. Each contains 4 ounces (½ cup) of semigloss alkyd enamel of the same color as the room's existing wood trim and 4 ounces (½ cup) of mineral spirits; the pale shadow requires 2 teaspoons of raw umber artist's paint, and the dark shadow requires both 2 teaspoons of raw umber artist's paint and 2 teaspoons of black.

Mix each color by first squeezing a 2-inch length (2 teaspoons) of each necessary artist's paint onto a broad saucer or a cleaned jar lid; add 1 ounce (2 tablespoons) of alkyd enamel. Stir the mix with a palette knife until it is smooth and creamy, then scrape it into a 10- to 12-ounce glass jar with a lid. Add the remaining enamel. With a spoon or mixing stick, stir until the mixture is uniform. Add mineral spirits and stir until the color is uniform.

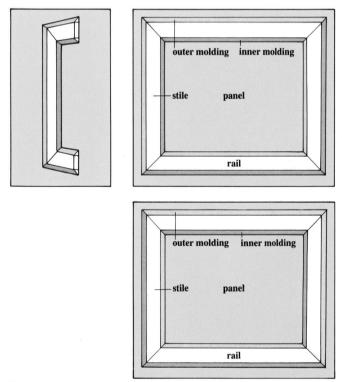

How to use shading colors. The molding on the stiles and rails that outline the panels shown above slants away from the panels in opposite directions. The inner moldings slant from the rails and stiles toward the panel; the outer moldings slant away from it. The molding that is directly in the path of light from the dominant source is comparatively pale in color. The molding that is in the shadows cast by the light source is darker. The panel at top shows how the shadows fall when the light emanates from above and to the left; the other panel shows the shadows cast by light from above and to the right.

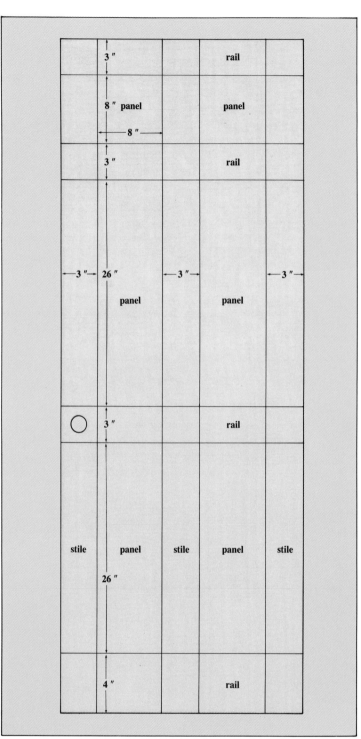

1 **Chalking a grid on the door.** Measure the height and width of your door, then make a scale drawing of the door on graph paper; include the placement of the doorknob. In a frame-and-panel door, the frame consists of vertical pieces called stiles and horizontal pieces called rails that enclose rectangular panels edged by molding. In the design here, the stiles, the top rail and the two rails below it are made of boards of equal width; the bottom rail is slightly wider. To transfer the grid to the door, lightly pencil marks at the top and bottom of the door to locate each vertical line, and at both sides of the door for each horizontal line. Using a chalk line, snap four vertical and six horizontal lines to form an outline of the fake panels (*above*).

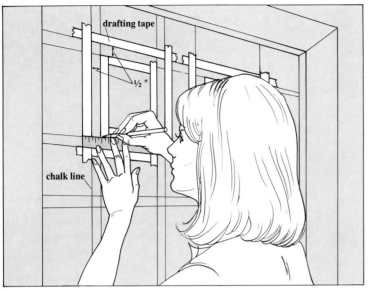

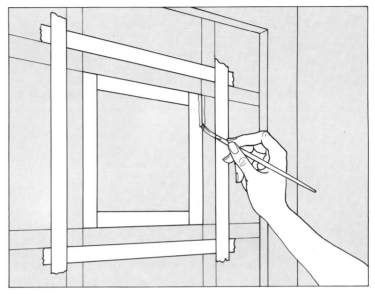

2 **Outlining the chalk lines with tape.** Apply pieces of 1-inch drafting tape to the door along the outside edges of the lines around the panels. Measure ½ inch toward the center of the panel from each of the two pairs of vertical chalk lines, mark the top and bottom of the door, and snap a chalk line between each set of marks. Repeat the process to snap chalk lines ½ inch inside each pair of existing horizontal chalk lines. Stick drafting tape along the inside edges of these ½-inch-wide spaces, which will simulate molding and will be shaded later. If ripped tape ends extend into the shading space, set a ruler's edge along the adjacent tape, lightly score the ragged end with an artist's knife, and gently tear away the tape *(above)*.

3 **Sealing the tape border.** With a ¼-inch artist's brush, paint along the tape borders *(above)*, using paint that matches the existing color of the door. If the border is uneven or marked by imperfections, dab on the paint with the tips of the brush bristles; use a stippling or dotting motion to assure a tight seal. Let the paint dry overnight. Leave the tape in place while you do the *trompe l'oeil* painting.

4 **Applying the shading.** Determine the source of light that illuminates the door. Here, the light is from overhead left. On every mock door panel, mark an X (for dark) on the tape along the sides where the light source will create shadows. With a ½-inch artist's brush and paler shading color, stroke parallel to the tape to paint the sides of the panel that will be in the path of the light source. At the corners where the paler color ends, make 45° diagonal strokes, angling the brush bristles to form mock mitered joints *(left)*. Then apply the darker shading color to give the effect of shadow to the other two sides of the panel. ▶

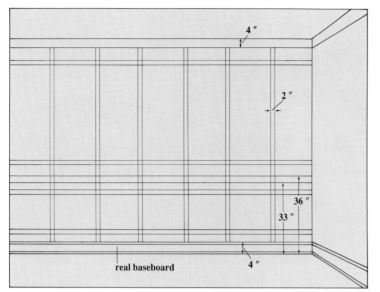

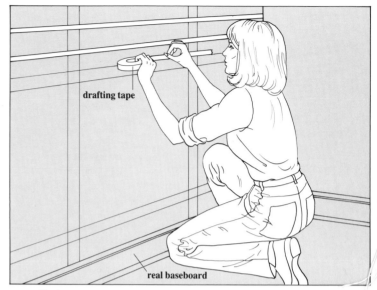

5 **Chalking a grid on the wall.** Make a scale drawing on graph paper of each wall; include doors, windows and existing trim. Then add the molding and paneling you want to simulate with paint. Here, the ceiling molding is 4 inches deep to match the wood baseboard. The chair rail is 3 inches deep and positioned 33 inches from the floor. The panels are centered between the rail and the floor and ceiling molding, and are spaced evenly across the wall. Their borders are 2 inches wide.

Transfer the graph-paper design to the wall as a grid of wall-to-wall and ceiling-to-floor chalk lines *(above)*.

6 **Taping the borders.** Apply 1-inch drafting tape along the ceiling at the wall-ceiling border, along the bottom of the ceiling-molding line, along both the top and bottom lines of the chair rail, and along the edges of the inner lines to form mock-panel borders 2 inches wide. Unroll the tape 10 to 12 inches at a time, smoothing it in place with your right thumbnail as you go *(above)*. Remove excess tape from the panel area with an artist's knife and a straightedge *(Step 2)*. Seal all of the tape with paint that matches the wall color *(Step 3)*.

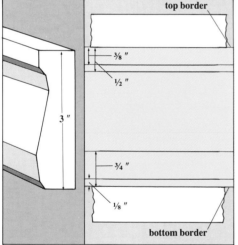

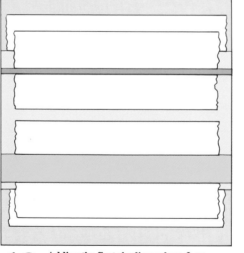

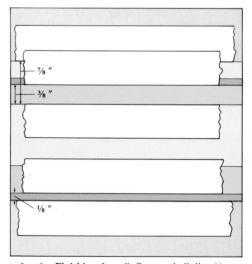

9 **Painting the chair rail.** Use the cross section of a chair rail at left as a guide to creating a *trompe l'oeil* rail, or draw a cross section of the molding you wish to simulate, adding shading to suggest its contours. Using a 2-inch brush, paint the strip between the sealed taped lines with two coats of semigloss alkyd enamel that matches the trim color. Let the paint dry for 24 hours after each coat. Snap chalk lines for the shading stripes: Here, the lines are ⅜ inch and ½ inch below the top border of the painted 3-inch-wide strip, and ⅛ inch and ¾ inch above the bottom border.

10 **Adding the first shading colors.** Lay 1-inch drafting tape along the outer edges of the newly made pairs of lines to form stripes at the top and bottom of the painted chair rail. Wipe off as much chalk as possible from the strip with a damp cloth, followed by a dry cloth. Mix the shading colors *(page 96)*. With a ½-inch round artist's brush, paint the upper stripe dark and the lower stripe light. Let the paint dry for several hours. Remove all the tapes except the bedded pieces along the borders.

11 **Finishing the rail.** Snap a chalk line ⅞ inch down from the top of the chair rail. Apply tape above the base of the upper shadow, covering the area. Lay another length below the new chalk line, and a third length above the base of the lower, lightly shaded area, covering it. Paint the ⅜-inch stripe between the top tapes with the pale shading color and the ⅛-inch stripe between the bottom tapes with dark shading *(above)*. Wait several hours before removing the tapes. Score the edges of the top and bottom border tapes with an artist's knife, then peel them off.

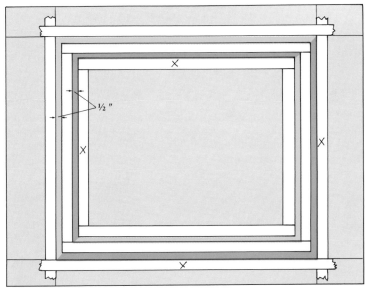

7 **Painting the mock panels.** Using a 2-inch China-bristle brush, paint the 2-inch borders between the tapes around the panels with a coat of semigloss alkyd enamel that matches any real wood trim in the room. Let the paint dry for 24 hours, then apply a second coat and wait 24 hours for the second coat to dry.

8 **Shading the panels.** Snap chalk lines ½ inch inside the outer borders of each wall panel to indicate the space for the shading. Lay 1-inch drafting tape inside the lines, leaving a second ½-inch space beside the inner borders. With an artist's knife *(Step 2),* remove excess tape inside the area to be painted. Determine the light source for your mock paneling: Here, the light emanates from overhead left. Mark an X on the tape next to the areas to receive the dark shading *(above).* Mix the paints, using the formulas described in the box on page 96. Paint the borders around the panels with a ½-inch artist's brush, angling the mitered corners where the two shades meet *(Step 4).*

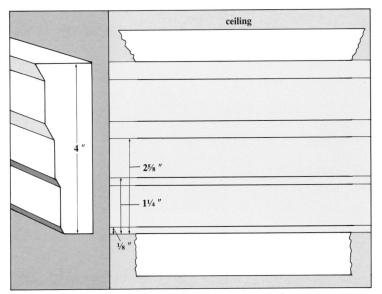

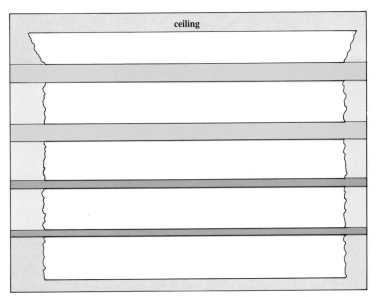

12 **Painting the ceiling molding.** Use the cross section of the molding above, at left, as a guide to creating mock molding at the ceiling, or draw a cross section of the molding you wish to simulate and add shading to suggest the contours. Since few ceilings are perfectly smooth, use the pale shading color where the ceiling and wall meet, to avoid drawing attention there. After bedding the tape delineating the bottom edge of the mock molding, give the wall above the tape two coats of semigloss alkyd enamel that matches the existing trim. Let both coats dry for 24 hours. Then snap chalk lines to mark the shading areas — in this case, the lines are ⅛ inch, 1¼ inches and 2⅝ inches above the tape.

13 **Adding shading at the ceiling.** Lay 1-inch drafting tape above each chalk line. Each length of tape will serve as the bottom of one shading area and the top of another. Mix the shading colors *(page 96).* Using a ½-inch round artist's brush, paint the upper stripes with the pale shading color and the lower stripes with the dark one. Let the paint dry for 24 hours. Gently score the hardened layers of paint along the tape borders with an artist's knife, then peel off the tape. Erase any leftover chalk lines with a damp cloth.

Paneling with solid wood

Walls sheathed in natural wood, like the knotty-pine tongue-and-groove boards in the photograph below, have enduring charm. And, surprisingly, wood paneling can rival wallpaper in economy and ease of installation.

Traditionally, paneling of this kind is installed vertically, as shown, but the boards may be mounted diagonally *(page 104)* or even horizontally *(page 107)*. Furring strips nailed horizontally to the studs provide a secure foundation for vertical and diagonal paneling; horizontal paneling may be nailed directly to the studs.

Because the paneling is about ¾ inch thick and the furring and paneling combined equal almost 1½ inches, the casings around doors and windows, and the stools and aprons on windows, must be removed before the paneling is installed. Afterward, the jambs can be extended *(page 104, Step 1)* to bring the openings flush with the new wall surface. Baseboards, chair rails, ceiling molding and the like must also be taken off by the technique on page 87 and replaced as described on pages 88-93.

To determine the number of feet of straight, knot-free 1-by-3 to buy for furring, multiply the room's perimeter by the number of horizontal rows of furring you will need — usually four *(diagram, page 102)*. For each pair of vertical furring strips in the corners, add twice the room's height. Add as well the perimeter of each door and window.

The number of board feet of paneling to buy depends on the installation pattern you choose and the board width and length, which can vary. For a vertical installation, get boards of one length to spare fitting problems, but for diagonal and horizontal installations, you may butt boards of different lengths end to end to minimize waste. Figure the area of the walls in square feet, and ask the lumber dealer how to order the boards most sensibly. To reduce the dangers of shrinkage and stretching later, let the new boards adjust for two days to the temperature and humidity in the room where they will be installed.

For a smooth finish, blind-nail the boards, that is, nail through the base of a board's tongue into the furring; the groove of the succeeding board will hide the nails. Right-handed people should install the boards from left to right, the tongues facing right, as shown on the following pages. Left-handers reverse the procedure, working right to left with tongues facing left.

A handsaw will suffice for crosscuts, but a circular saw, or a table saw, is faster and almost a necessity for ripping boards lengthwise. To install the boards straight and true, use a level, a plumb bob with a chalk line, a carpenter's square and a combination square. Fasten the boards with eightpenny finishing nails, sinking any heads that show with a nail set and filling the depressions with wood putty.

After installing the paneling, smooth it with medium (100-grit), then fine (150-grit) sandpaper, and apply wood stain and varnish, or penetrating oil.

Preparing Windows and Doors

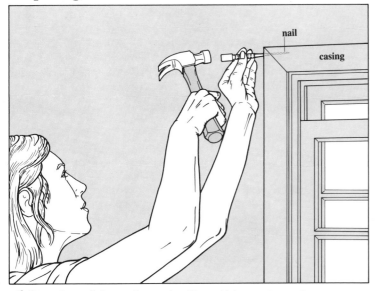

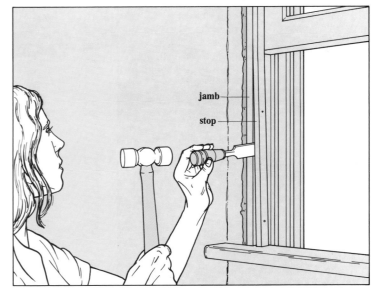

1 **Removing a window or door casing.** To avoid damage to a casing you are planning to reuse, first locate the nail that locks each of the mitered corners of the casing. Use a nail set to drive each nail beyond the corner joint *(above)*. Then use a utility knife to slit the paint seal between the wall and the sides and top of the casing and — for a window — the apron or trim below the stool. Carefully pry off the casing and apron, using the technique shown for a baseboard on page 87. Save all of the woodwork you are going to reuse.

2 **Prying off the stops.** If the window has a stool, remove the interior stops on each side: Score the joint between the stop and the jamb with a utility knife to break the paint seal. Starting at the bottom, set a chisel between stop and jamb, the beveled edge of the chisel against the jamb. Tapping the chisel with a mallet, work up the stop to pry it away from the jamb *(above)*. Repeat the procedure to remove the other side stop. Save the stops if you plan to reuse them.

3 **Removing the window stool.** Drive the nails that secure the horns of the stool to the window frame completely through the wood, as in Step 1. Using a pry bar, pry up the stool along its back edge; work from one end of the window to the other and protect its sill by keeping a wood scrap under the back of the pry bar. Save the stool to use as a pattern for cutting a new one *(page 104, Step 2)*.

Installing Boards Vertically

A wall of interlocking boards. Tongue-and-groove paneling boards fit into each other side by side *(page 83),* and hidden nails driven through their tongues hold them to a base of 1-by-3 furring strips. The horizontal furring strips are set along the floor and ceiling and at approximately 3-foot intervals between, and are attached to the wall studs with eightpenny nails. Vertical strips stabilize the boards at inside and outside corners. Furring also surrounds the window and door openings.

Before the boards are fastened to the furring on each wall, measures are taken to prevent the last board on the wall from ending up a narrow strip: The wall width is divided by the width of a board exclusive of its tongue. The remainder is added to a full board width and the sum divided by 2. The first board is then ripped (sawed lengthwise) to this width, and the grooved edge discarded. The last board on the wall, which is cut to fit when installed, will end up nearly the same width as the first board.

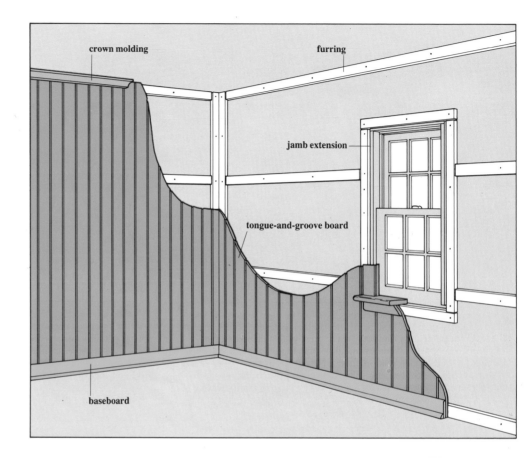

3 **Fitting boards around an opening.** Install the first board that overlaps an opening, but do not nail it. Mark the opening's top and bottom furring strips where the edge of the board's tongue crosses them, then mark the underside of the tongue where the inner edges of these strips meet it. Remove the board. Measure from the marks on the top and bottom furring strips to the inner edge of the nearest side strip. At the marks on the board's tongue, draw lines of these lengths perpendicular to the tongue. Connect the ends of the two lines with one parallel to the tongue *(inset).* Cut out a notch along the lines with a saber saw, and blind-nail the board to the furring. Measure and cut short boards to fit above and below the opening. Then cut a board to fit the opening's other side.

4 **Enclosing an electric fixture.** Turn off the power to the room at the main switch box. Remove the cover plate and the screws holding a switch or — as here — an outlet in its box, and pull out the fixture about 1 inch. Slide a box extender over the fixture and into the box; screw the fixture loosely to the extender. Hold a board in place without nailing it, and mark horizontal lines on the board just above and below the screw brackets at the top and bottom of the fixture. Connect the marks with a vertical line that will clear the side edge of the fixture's box. Cut a notch along the lines with a saber saw, then install the board. Mark, cut and install the next board in the same way. Bring the outlets flush with the face of the paneling by adjusting the screws.

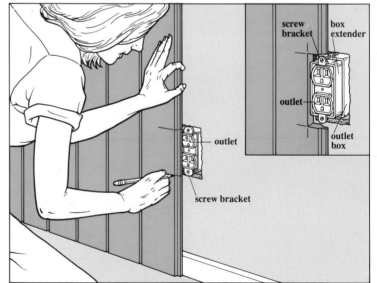

1 **Plumbing the first board.** Measure the wall and cut the first board, if necessary, as explained opposite. Set the board flat against the wall with its grooved edge in the corner. Tap eightpenny finishing nails partway into the face of the board, 1 inch from the grooved edge, at two of the horizontal furring strips. Check for plumb with a carpenter's level *(left),* moving the board from side to side. When the board is vertical, drive the two nails, and sink their heads with a nail set. Face-nail the board into the remaining horizontal furring strips.

2 **Blind-nailing the board.** Drive an eight-penny finishing nail at a 45° angle through the base of the tongue into each horizontal furring strip *(right, inset).* Sink the heads with a nail set. Fit the groove of each succeeding board over the tongue of the previous board. The fit may be snug, but do not jam the boards tightly together. Blind-nail each board as you proceed and check every third board for verticality.

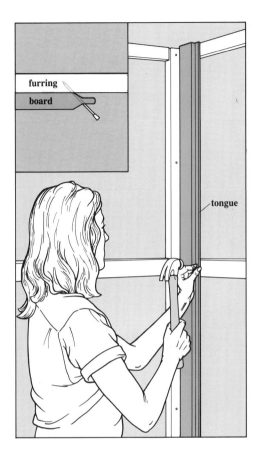

5 **Installing boards at an inside corner.** Hold the second-to-last board in place without nailing it. Measure to the inside corner from the base of the tongue of the second-to-last board, and cut the last board to that width, discarding the tongued edge. Pull the tongued edge of the second-to-last board away from the wall, slip on the grooved edge of the final board and push in the joint to lock the boards *(above).* Face-nail the boards with two nails at each horizontal furring strip, 1 inch from the tongued edge and 1 inch from the grooved edge *(inset).*

Rounding an Outside Corner

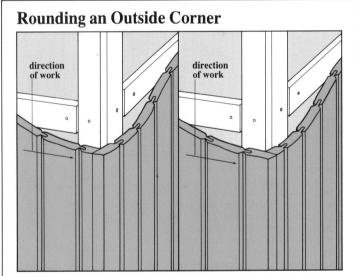

To panel an outside corner neatly, cut off the tongued edge of the last board on one wall so the right-hand edge of the board fits flush with the corner *(left, above);* face-nail the board at the horizontal furring-strip positions. Measure the next wall to determine the width for the first and last boards *(opposite, top),* and cut the groove off the first board for the wall. Face-nail it to the furring, its cut edge flush with the face of the preceding board. Alternatively, you can cut the last board so that it extends one board thickness beyond the corner and butt the cut edge of the next board against its back *(above, right).* Trim the exposed cut edges of the boards with a block plane to make them smooth and even with the face of the adjoining board.

Replacing Window and Door Trim

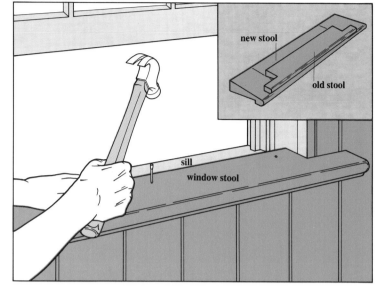

1 **Extending the jambs.** To bring the top and side jambs of a window or door flush with the paneling, make jamb extensions: Measure from the jamb to the surface of the paneling and cut three strips from nominal 1-inch lumber of this width. Attach first the top, then the side extensions to the front edges of the jambs with wood glue and finishing nails of the appropriate length.

2 **Installing a new window stool.** Cut a new stool, using the old stool as a pattern but extending its back edge so it will fit from the jamb extensions to the window sash *(inset)*. Drill a ⅛-inch pilot hole near each corner of the stool at a point that will be hidden by the side stop, and at three points, evenly spaced, 1 inch from the back edge. Position the stool in the window frame and drive eightpenny finishing nails through the pilot holes into the sill. Recess the nailheads.

Installing Boards Diagonally

Tongue-and-groove paneling boards, positioned at a 45° angle, are nailed through their tongues into a foundation of 1-by-3 furring strips installed the same way as for vertical paneling *(diagram, page 102)*. The boards' ends are cut at a 45° angle to fit flush with the ceiling, floor and corners. To cover a tall wall, boards may be butted and glued together at a horizontal furring strip, then face-nailed into the furring there.

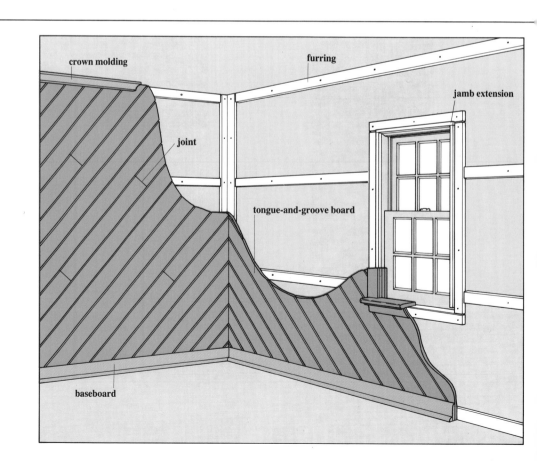

3 **Installing the casing.** Reuse the original casings and apron, if you like, or make new ones. Cut a new top casing, its ends mitered at a 45° angle *(page 93, Step 3),* to fit along the head jamb ⅛ inch from the inner edge. Tack the ends of the casing to the jamb with fourpenny finishing nails. Then — starting from one end — nail through the casing into the jamb at 12-inch intervals, inserting fourpenny finishing nails ¼ inch from the bottom edge of the casing and sixpenny finishing nails ½ inch from the top edge. Cut two side casings to fit between the mitered ends of the top casing and the horns of the stool, and nail them the same way. Lock-nail the corner joints *(inset)* to tighten them. Cut an apron to fit beneath the stool and nail it in place.

4 **Replacing the side stops.** Reinstall the original side stops if they are in good condition. If not, cut new stops, coping their top ends to fit against the head stop *(page 91, Steps 10-11)* if the moldings are contoured. Place each stop against the window sash and tack it to the side jamb. Open and close the window to see if the sash binds or rattles; reposition the stops if necessary. Nail the side stops in place with fourpenny finishing nails spaced 12 inches apart.

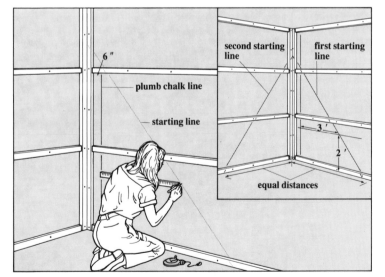

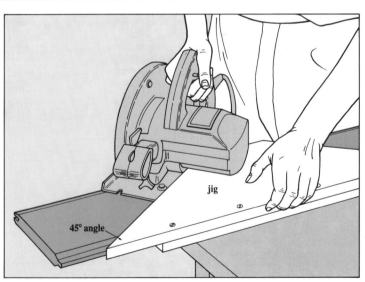
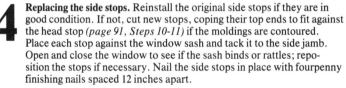
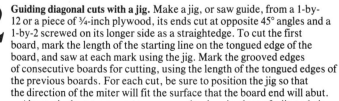

1 **Laying out a 45° starting line.** Snap a plumb chalk line from the ceiling to the floor about 6 inches from one corner of a wall. Make tick marks 2 feet from the floor at the chalk line and several feet away from it. Using a yardstick, draw a horizontal line connecting the marks *(above).* Then mark each line 3 feet from their intersection and connect these marks by snapping a diagonal chalk line extending from corner to floor. At the floor line, measure from the bottom of the starting line to the corner. To establish a starting line on the adjoining wall, make a mark at the floor line the same distance from the corner as the bottom of the first starting line. Snap a diagonal chalk line between this mark and the top of the first starting line *(inset).*

2 **Guiding diagonal cuts with a jig.** Make a jig, or saw guide, from a 1-by-12 or a piece of ¾-inch plywood, its ends cut at opposite 45° angles and a 1-by-2 screwed on its longer side as a straightedge. To cut the first board, mark the length of the starting line on the tongued edge of the board, and saw at each mark using the jig. Mark the grooved edges of consecutive boards for cutting, using the length of the tongued edges of the previous boards. For each cut, be sure to position the jig so that the direction of the miter will fit the surface that the board end will abut.

Alternatively, you may use a power miter box in place of a jig and circular saw to make the mitered cuts. ▶

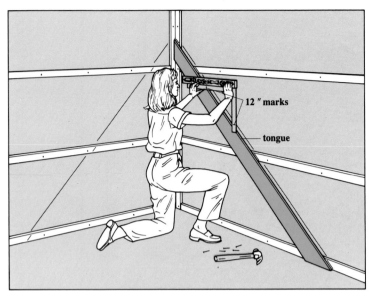

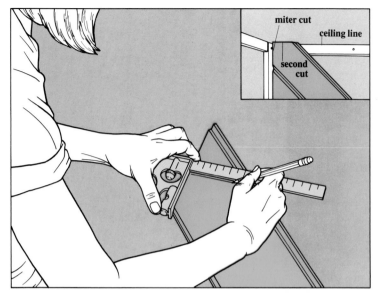

3 **Maintaining a 45° angle.** Check the angle of the first board and every third board after you position it: Hold a carpenter's square against the board, lining up the two 12-inch marks on the square with the tongued edge. Hold a level on the horizontal arm of the square and adjust the board until the arm is level, then blind-nail the board *(page 103, Step 2).*

4 **Measuring double-angle cuts.** When one end of a board will butt two surfaces — such as the ceiling or floor and a wall corner *(inset)* — first miter the end to fit the corner. Then measure how much of the corner remains to be covered by the board, and mark this distance on the mitered end, measuring from the grooved edge if the board butts the ceiling and from the tongued edge if it butts the floor. Use a combination square to draw a perpendicular line from the mark to the opposite edge of the board *(above);* cut along the line.

Beveling Boards for an Outside Corner

To install the first diagonal board that meets the corner, miter both ends and position the board without nailing. Draw a line across the back of the board where it crosses the corner. Lay the board face down. Set the blade of a circular saw at a 45° angle and cut the board along the line, angling the cut toward the waste end of the board. Install the board so that the back edge of the compound miter is even with the corner *(inset)*, and nail the board in place.

On subsequent boards, miter only the top end. Position the board, mark its back where it crosses the corner, and cut the miter along this line. At the top corner, glue and face-nail the small triangular last board.

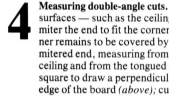

equal measurements

tongue

face nails

5 **Fitting diagonal boards around an opening.** Miter-cut the ends of the first board that overlaps the corner of a door or window, and fit the board in place. Check its angle *(Step 3)*, then mark the back of the board where its edge crosses the furring strips. Remove the board and use a carpenter's square to draw a right-angle notch between the two marks *(inset)*. Cut out the angle with a saber saw, then nail the board in place.

6 **Installing shorter boards.** Working down from the starting board, miter the boards to fit, using the grooved edge of the previous board as a measure. Since the tongued edge will be hidden, you will have to face-nail these boards to the furring, with two eightpenny nails 1 inch from each end and two nails wherever a board crosses a horizontal furring strip. On the boards near the bottom corner, trim several inches from each end of the tongue with a utility knife; this makes it easier to work the tongue into the groove of the board above. Anchor the triangular last board with wood glue as well as nails. Short boards near the top corner should be face-nailed an inch from each end, and the last board glued.

A Horizontal Installation

If the wall is in good condition, tongue-and-groove boards may be nailed horizontally directly to the studs, eliminating the need for furring. Vertical chalk lines mark the stud locations *(page 19)*. Baseboards *(page 87)* and door and window casings *(page 101, Step 1)* are removed as for furred paneling; however, the window stool may remain in place and the boards be cut to fit around it.

So that the topmost board on the wall is full width, the height of the wall is divided by the board width minus the tongue. The bottom board then is ripped, or sawed lengthwise, to the width of the remainder, and the grooved edge is discarded.

The bottom board is installed first, its ripped edge resting on the floor. One end of the board is raised and lowered until a level shows that it is horizontal; the board is face-nailed into each stud with an eightpenny finishing nail.

Successive boards are fitted one atop the other and blind-nailed at the studs; every third board is checked for level. The tongue is cut off the topmost board before it is installed. Short boards are trimmed to meet at a stud; their ends are glued together and then face-nailed to the stud. Board ends are butted at both inside and outside corners.

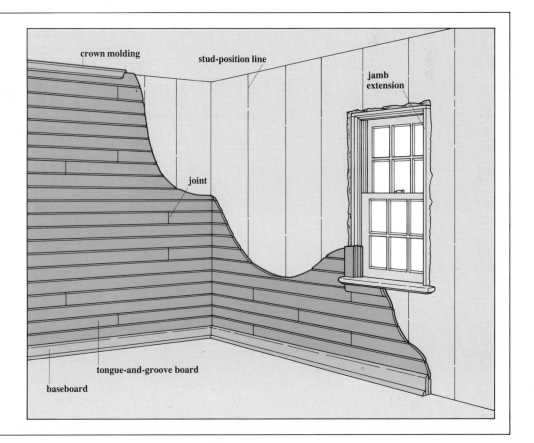

crown molding

stud-position line

jamb extension

joint

tongue-and-groove board

baseboard

Paneling with plywood

Handsome plywood paneling can bring the warmth of wood to a room at far less cost than solid wood boards. The most elegant of the panels consist of laminations of inexpensive wood with a veneer of fine wood; panels of simulated wood grain printed on paper and mounted on plywood or hardboard *(chart, page 81)* are even more economical.

Because the panels are so large — 4 by 8 feet or 4 by 10 feet — the effect they create is easy to gauge quickly. And the work goes quickly if you have conventional walls that are flat and smooth: The panels can be attached directly to plaster or wall-board, using paneling adhesive and special paneling nails colored to match the plywood finish. If your walls are out of square or have extensive surface damage, or if they are masonry, you need a grid of furring strips to provide a base for the paneling *(page 113)*.

To estimate how many panels you need, measure the total width in feet of the walls in the room and divide by 4. Store the panels in the room where they will be used for at least 48 hours before installing them; this allows the wood to adjust to the room's temperature and humidity, reducing the danger of the wood expanding after the panels are installed. If the panels have a real-wood veneer with random graining, stand them against the wall and arrange them in an order that suits your taste before you begin installation. Printed panels are nearly identical and can be installed in almost any order.

The panels are installed one at a time — each panel is individually fitted, cut and attached. With a 4-foot level and a straight board roughly equivalent to the height of the walls, you can detect any juts or valleys in the wall surface or any slant to the ceiling *(Step 2)*, and can compensate for it so that your first corner panel — the key to the appearance of your entire project — will be perfectly plumb

(Step 5). Thereafter, succeeding panels are butted against each other. The trickiest part of installing them is cutting and fitting panels around interruptions in the wall, such as doors, windows, electrical switches and outlets.

Both plywood and hardboard panels can be readily cut. For long straight cuts, use a fine-toothed crosscut handsaw or a portable circular saw fitted with a plywood blade that has six teeth per inch. For short straight cuts and curved cuts, use a keyhole saw or a saber saw with 10 teeth per inch. Circular and saber saws have an advantage in that they cut on the upstroke, allowing you to mark cutting lines on the back of each panel and confine most of the splinters from the cut to that surface. With handsaws, mark the finished side of the panel and cut with that side facing up.

The paneling adhesive, a caulking gun to apply it *(Step 4),* and paneling nails are sold by panel suppliers. You will need one 11-ounce tube of adhesive for every three panels. If you are installing the panels directly onto plaster or wallboard, use 1⅝-inch nails to attach them to the wall studs. If you are installing them on a grid of furring strips or directly onto uncovered studs, use 1-inch nails.

To keep installed prefinished plywood panels looking new, wipe them occasionally with a cloth lightly dampened in a mild detergent solution. If you have finished the plywood panels yourself, or if you have hardwood panels, treat them as you would fine furniture — with a cleaner designed specially for hardwood.

Minor scratches can be concealed by a matching wood stain applied with a rag or brush, or by colored wax rubbed into them with a cloth. For deep blemishes, some manufacturers offer putty sticks that match the color of their panels.

Over the years, exposure to light and air may cause some panels to fade, leaving the areas hidden behind pictures looking conspicuously darker. To minimize this problem, stick pushpins or tacks into the back of each picture frame to create a ½-inch air space behind it. The space will help the covered area age at more or less the same rate as the rest of the wall.

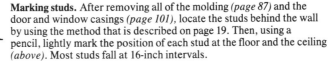

1 **Marking studs.** After removing all of the molding *(page 87)* and the door and window casings *(page 101),* locate the studs behind the wall by using the method that is described on page 19. Then, using a pencil, lightly mark the position of each stud at the floor and the ceiling *(above).* Most studs fall at 16-inch intervals.

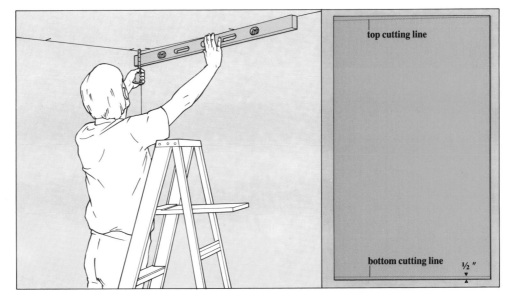

2 **Measuring cutting lines.** Slide a straight board roughly equal to the wall height along the wall to check for juts or valleys. If you find any that are more than ½ inch, correct the surface with furring strips *(page 113).* Then hold a 4-foot-long level against the top of the wall at a corner of the room to check whether the ceiling slants. If it does, measure the gap between the level and the ceiling at the ceiling's highest point *(above).* Next, measure the distance from ceiling to floor at the corner of the room and 4 feet away from the corner. Subtract ½ inch from both measurements (molding will later cover this space). Then measure the distance of the ceiling gap on one side of the panel and draw a cutting line from that point to the panel's opposite corner. If you are using a power saw, mark the cutting line on the back of the panel; for a handsaw, mark the front side. Then measure from the top cutting line (or from the top of the panel if the ceiling does not slope) and draw a bottom cutting line. ▶

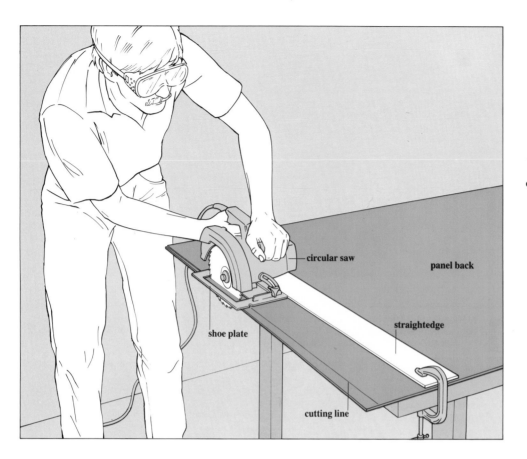

3 **Trimming the panel.** Place the panel on a worktable allowing just enough overhang for the saw to clear the table. (With too much overhang, the plywood will bend and may crack.) If you use a handsaw, cut with the finished side of the panel up.

If you are using a circular saw, lay the panel face down to avoid splintering the wood. Set the saw on the panel so that the inside of the blade falls on the waste side of the cutting line. Clamp a straightedge to the panel against the inner edge of the saw's shoe plate. Put on goggles, then saw along the cutting line.

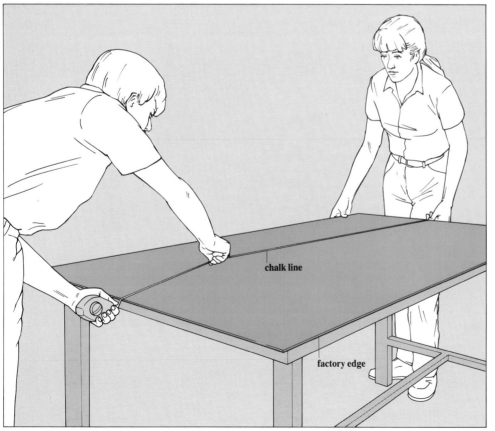

6 **Marking a corner.** Trim the next corner panel to the proper height *(Steps 2-3)*. Then determine its proper width by measuring from the corner of the room to the edge of the last panel installed at both the ceiling and floor. Mark these distances on the corner panel's top and bottom edges so that the factory-cut edge will fall against the panel already in place.

Lay the panel on a worktable and snap a chalk line between the marks *(left)*. Then cut along the line using the circular saw, with the straightedge board as a guide. Install the cut panel as you did the full-width panels. If the fit is too tight, shave the cut edge with a block plane until it fits against the corner. Continue paneling the next wall.

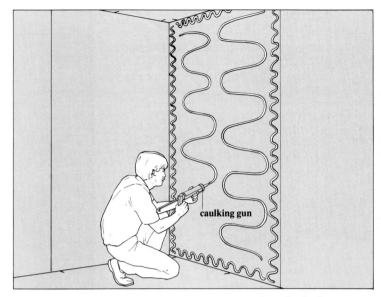

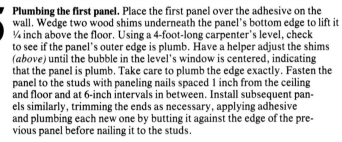

4 **Applying adhesive.** Fit an 11-ounce tube of paneling adhesive into a caulking gun. With a utility knife, cut off the tip of the tube at a 45° angle. Beginning at the top of the corner of the room, outline the wall area that will be covered by the first panel with a wavy, continuous bead of glue. Then fill in the area between with several serpentine beads that extend from the ceiling to the floor (*above*).

5 **Plumbing the first panel.** Place the first panel over the adhesive on the wall. Wedge two wood shims underneath the panel's bottom edge to lift it ¼ inch above the floor. Using a 4-foot-long carpenter's level, check to see if the panel's outer edge is plumb. Have a helper adjust the shims (*above*) until the bubble in the level's window is centered, indicating that the panel is plumb. Take care to plumb the edge exactly. Fasten the panel to the studs with paneling nails spaced 1 inch from the ceiling and floor and at 6-inch intervals in between. Install subsequent panels similarly, trimming the ends as necessary, applying adhesive and plumbing each new one by butting it against the edge of the previous panel before nailing it to the studs.

7 **Paneling around a window.** When you near a window or door, first plumb and trim a panel to the proper height (*Steps 2-3*). At two or three points along the window's width, measure between the ceiling and the top of the window frame and between the floor and the bottom of the frame. Subtract ¼ inch from both measurements. Then measure from the last panel installed to the vertical edge of the frame. Transfer these measurements to the panel.

Using a pencil and straightedge to connect the points, outline the section to be cut out. Saw with the inside of the blade on the waste side of the outline.

Stand the panel in place and make light pencil marks on it to indicate the position of the window's stool, or inner sill. Take the panel down, draw an outline of the sill on the panel (*inset*) and cut it out with a saber saw. Apply adhesive and install the panel. Handle the other side of the window or door in the same way. ▶

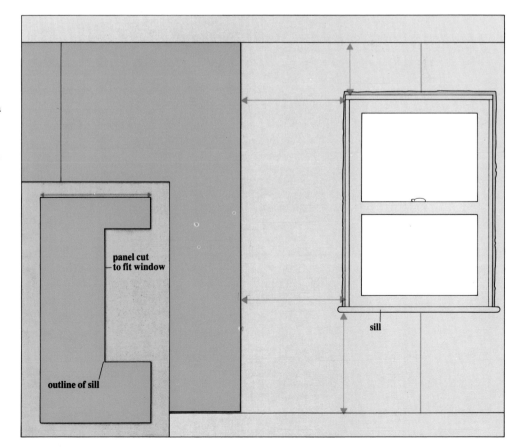

8 **Making small cutouts.** When you near an electric receptacle or switch plate or a wall-mounted register, shut off the power to the room at the main switch. With a screwdriver, remove the protective cover to expose the receptacle, switch or register. Measure from the floor to the edge of the opening and from the edge of the nearest installed panel to the edge of the opening *(inset)*. Using these measurements, and measurements that correspond to the size of the opening, mark the four corners of the opening on the panel.

Drive small nails through the panel to make holes at each corner of the outline. Remove the nails. Turn the panel over and drill ¾-inch holes just inside the four corners of the outline. Then use a keyhole saw *(right)* or saber saw to cut the outline. If you use a keyhole saw, mark and cut from the front of the panel; for a saber saw, mark and cut from the back of the panel. The cutout can be up to ¼ inch oversize and still be covered when the protective plate is replaced. Install the plywood panel. Use extenders, available at hardware stores, to adjust the outlets or switches; install registers directly over the panel, using longer screws if necessary. Finally, replace the protective plate.

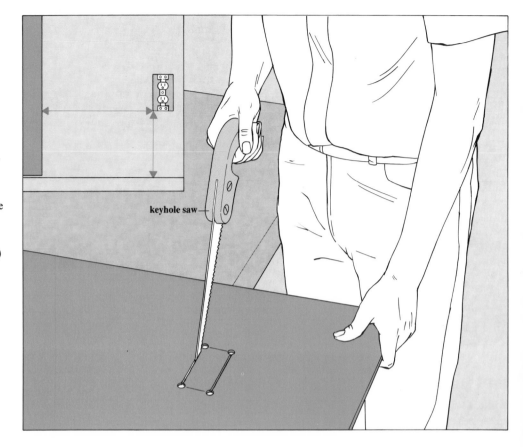
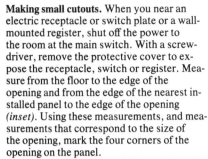

keyhole saw

9 **Attaching corner moldings.** Install moldings at the ceiling and baseboard *(pages 88-93)*. Then butt the ends of an appropriately shaped corner molding — L-shaped for an outside corner, slightly concave for an inside one — between the baseboard and ceiling moldings. Fasten the corner molding to the panels with fourpenny finishing nails spaced 2 inches from the top and bottom and at 12-inch intervals between. For an inside corner, drive the nails into the center of the molding *(right)*. For an outside corner, drive the nails through alternate sides into the studs backing the panel *(inset)*.

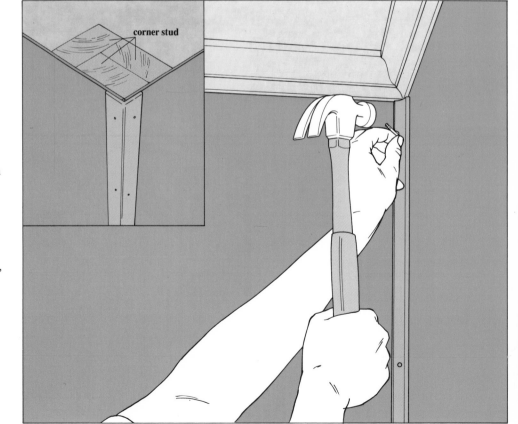

corner stud

A Grid of Furring Strips

Walls that have bumps or are seriously out of plumb can be paneled with plywood, too. But the panels require a smooth, flat base created by nailing to the wall a grid of furring strips cut from 1-by-2 and 1-by-4 lumber, as shown here.

To prepare for the grid, all moldings and door and window trim are removed *(page 101)*, and door and window jambs are extended to accommodate the combined thickness of grid and paneling — a total of 1 inch. The depth of electric switch and outlet boxes also must be increased with box extenders.

At this stage the stud locations are marked at ceiling and floor *(page 109, Step 1)*. Two 1-by-4s cut to fit across the wall are loosely attached at the ceiling and floor by eightpenny nails at each end and in the center. A straight board roughly equal to the height of the wall is then held on edge along the face of one 1-by-4. Working back and forth across the wall, the 1-by-4 is shimmed out — by inserting shim shingles or wedge-shaped pieces of wood — until it is as straight as the guide board. The other 1-by-4 is shimmed in the same way, then the guide board and a level are held vertically to see that the faces of the two 1-by-4s are level. If not, the deeper one is shimmed further. Both 1-by-4s are now secured tightly to the wall at the studs with eightpenny finishing nails, and all shims are nailed in place.

The next steps are marking locations along two adjacent stud lines for horizontal 1-by-2s at 16-inch intervals and cutting enough 1-by-2s the width of the wall. Before these are set in place, the guide board is held vertically against the 1-by-4s and a scrap of 1-by-2 slid behind it. If the scrap slides easily, the 1-by-2s can simply be nailed up. If there is a gap of ⅛ inch or more, the horizontal 1-by-2s are shimmed as they are installed. And if the scrap does not pass under the board, one 1-by-2 is installed where the gap is narrowest. Now the 1-by-4 at the ceiling must be re-leased and shimmed again until it is level with the 1-by-2; then the remaining 1-by-2 horizontals are nailed in place.

Finally, short vertical 1-by-2s are nailed over the stud lines, shimmed where necessary to lie flush with the horizontal 1-by-2s. Additional 1-by-2s frame the corners, windows and doors, and a strip spanning two studs supports the paneling around an electric outlet.

Now panels are sized, trimmed and installed, starting from the corner. First, panel adhesive is applied in a continuous bead to the top, side and bottom furring strips that will outline the panel's edges — and more adhesive is applied in 3-inch-long beads 6 inches apart on the remaining intermediate strips.

The panel is then positioned, shimmed and leveled *(page 111, Step 5)* before it is pressed into place. All four edges are nailed to furring strips with fourpenny nails, then a row of nails is put down the panel center into the horizontal strips.

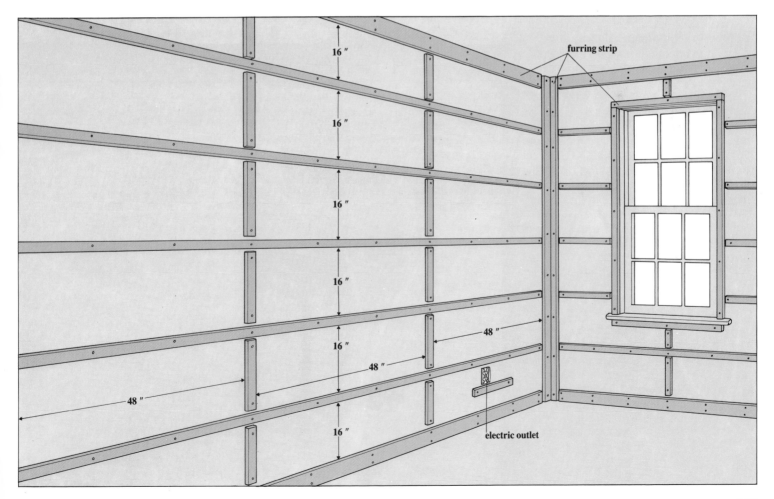

The old-fashioned charm of wainscots

All types of wall treatments, from *trompe l'oeil* images to plywood sheets, can be adjusted to create wainscoting: a classic decorative device to differentiate the lower one third to one half of a wall from the rest.

Generally, wainscots are formed with wood, as shown here. The casual, country look of the seemingly narrow strips of wood at top right is produced by 1-by-4 beaded tongue-and-groove porch ceiling boards installed in the same fashion as the floor-to-ceiling paneling on pages 100-103. Any of the alternative boards on pages 82-83 could be used instead, to give other effects.

The boards are 36 inches long — one third the height of the walls in this room. Their length can be varied to suit the proportions of a room — or to meet architectural features such as a window sill or a countertop.

A standard wood molding called wainscot cap — available in a variety of styles — fits over the upper edge of the installed boards. If — as in the example — the wainscot cap is too narrow to extend over the full width of the boards plus the furring behind them, the cap may be widened by gluing another strip of wood to its back edge. Or a wainscot cap can be custom-designed by assembling several stock moldings, as with the chair rail on page 93.

The more formal wainscot at bottom right is composed of standard dimension lumber trimmed with molding to frame rectangles of blank wall. Painting the boards and the wall the same color unifies the different elements.

All of the pieces for the frames are cut and fastened by the techniques shown on pages 88-92. First, the rectangles are plotted and marked on the wall. The horizontal 1-by-10s are installed like baseboard, cut square and butted at the corners *(pages 88-89)*. The horizontal 1-by-8s above them are positioned by the method used for the rectangles on page 92. Vertical 1-by-6s complete the rectangles, which then are trimmed with ogee cap molding, mitered at the corners and fastened as demonstrated on page 90. The top board is trimmed with wainscot cap molding.

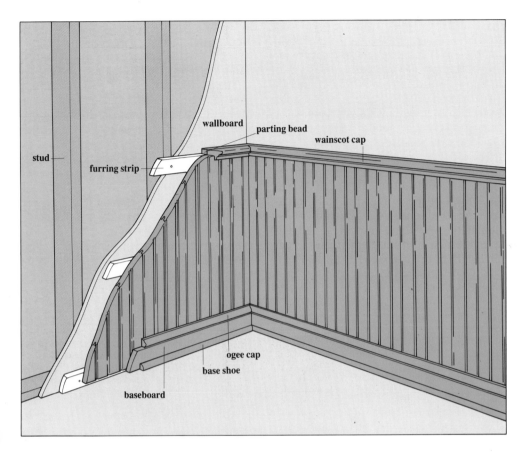

Tongue-and-groove wainscoting. Three horizontal rows of 1-by-3 furring are nailed to the studs with sixpenny finishing nails to provide a base for the paneling. Blind nailing *(page 103, Step 2)* secures 1-by-4 tongue-and-groove ceiling boards 36 inches long to the furring. The baseboard consists of a 1-by-4 trimmed with quarter-round base shoe molding and ogee cap molding. Wainscot cap molding — widened with a strip of ½-by-¾-inch parting bead that has been glued and nailed to its back edge with 1¼-inch brads — conceals the top of the uppermost furring strip and the top edges of the tongue-and-groove boards. The wainscot cap is attached with sixpenny finishing nails spaced 12 inches apart and driven through the boards into the furring strip.

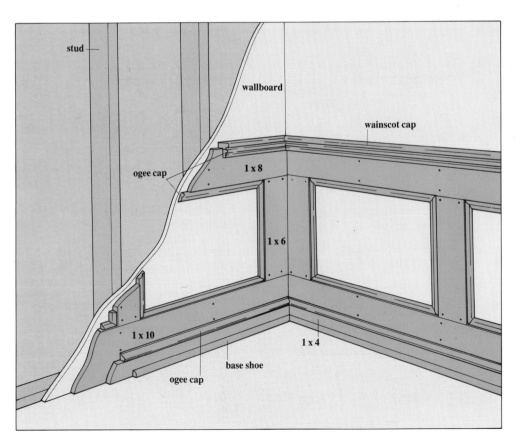

A grid of boards. At the floor line, a 1-by-10 is fastened to the wall with sixpenny finishing nails driven into the studs; in the corners of the room, the board butts against matching 1-by-10s. A 1-by-8 — its top edge set parallel to the 1-by-10 and 36 inches above the floor — is nailed similarly to the studs. Lengths of 1-by-6, cut to fit vertically between the horizontal boards, are attached at top and bottom to the edges of those boards with fourpenny finishing nails driven diagonally, or toenailed. A 1-by-4 baseboard, nailed to the face of the 1-by-10 with sixpenny finishing nails, is trimmed with base shoe and ogee cap moldings, both fastened with 1¼-inch brads. Ogee cap molding, also fastened with 1¼-inch brads, trims the inside edges of the rectangles formed by the larger boards. Wainscot cap molding fits over the top edge of the 1-by-8 and is nailed in place with fourpenny finishing nails spaced 12 inches apart and driven down through the top.

An adaptable design for radiator covers

Ever since the invention of radiators, people have been trying to make them disappear. The most direct disguise is to conceal them beneath wood covers, thus improving the look of a room for anyone who prefers the sight of cabinetwork to a view of the plumbing.

The radiator cover below, top, and diagramed opposite is a straightforward piece of carpentry that can be built in an afternoon — and adapted easily to fit a variety of décors. The three additional illustrations below are examples of ways the cover's appearance can be altered.

The cover is constructed of stock lumber. All of the pieces except the horizontal facings — which must be trimmed to fit — can be precut. To determine what size boards you need, measure your radiator from its front face to the wall and add 1 inch. If the face stands 8 inches or less from the wall, use the materials listed opposite; if the face is 8 to 10 inches from the wall, use 1-by-12s for the sides and a 13¼-inch-wide strip of plywood for the top piece. For deeper radiators, use plywood side panels.

To calculate the height of the side panels and the stiles, measure the height of the radiator and add at least 1 inch. To get the length of the horizontal rails, measure the total length of the radiator, including the valve and any pipes, and add at least 1 inch; add another 4 inches to get the length of the top piece.

Buy kiln-dried select pine lumber; lesser grades have a greater tendency to warp when subjected to heat. Kiln-dried hardwoods such as cherry or maple are good, though costlier, alternatives. If you are using plywood, buy ¾-inch A2 grade.

The front section of the basic cover is a sheet of perforated metal screen, available at lumberyards and hardware stores. The screen comes in several patterns and sizes. Choose the size closest to that of the opening in your radiator cover, then trim the sheet to fit with metal shears after you have constructed the wood frame.

The cover can be moved easily to adjust the heat. But if you adjust it frequently, you may want to cut an access notch in the side panel next to the valve. Finish the cover with any latex or alkyd paint or transparent wood finish that matches the walls or the woodwork in the room.

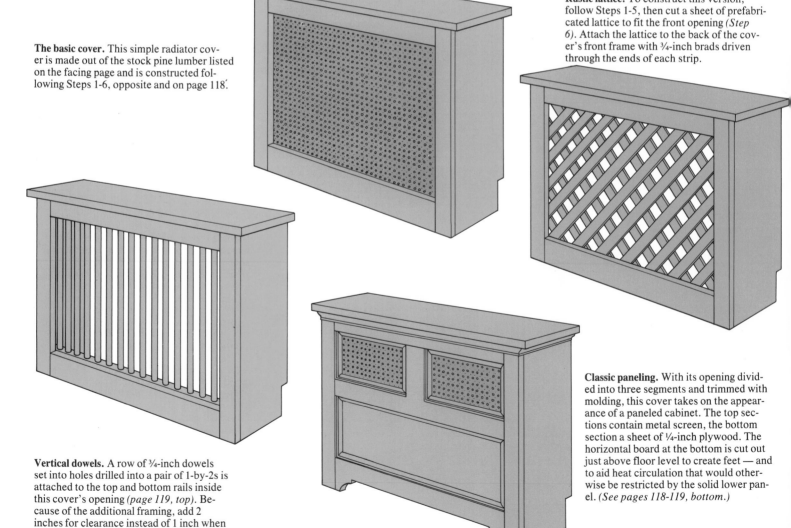

The basic cover. This simple radiator cover is made out of the stock pine lumber listed on the facing page and is constructed following Steps 1-6, opposite and on page 118.

Rustic lattice. To construct this version, follow Steps 1-5, then cut a sheet of prefabricated lattice to fit the front opening (*Step 6*). Attach the lattice to the back of the cover's front frame with ¾-inch brads driven through the ends of each strip.

Vertical dowels. A row of ¾-inch dowels set into holes drilled into a pair of 1-by-2s is attached to the top and bottom rails inside this cover's opening (*page 119, top*). Because of the additional framing, add 2 inches for clearance instead of 1 inch when measuring the depth of the radiator.

Classic paneling. With its opening divided into three segments and trimmed with molding, this cover takes on the appearance of a paneled cabinet. The top sections contain metal screen, the bottom section a sheet of ¼-inch plywood. The horizontal board at the bottom is cut out just above floor level to create feet — and to aid heat circulation that would otherwise be restricted by the solid lower panel. (*See pages 118-119, bottom.*)

Materials List

Lumber	1 select pine 1 x 12 top piece, cut the length of the radiator plus 4 ″
	2 select pine 1 x 10 side panels, cut the height of the radiator plus 1 ″
	1 select pine 1 x 4 bottom facing, cut to fit (approximately the length of the radiator)
	4 select pine 1 x 3s, cut into: 2 stiles the height of the side panels
	1 bottom rail the length of the radiator plus 1 ″
	1 top facing, cut to fit (approximately the length of the radiator)
	1 select pine 1 x 2, cut into 1 top rail the length of the radiator plus 1 ″
Screen	1 sheet perforated metal screen
Hardware	14 No. 8 flat-head wood screws, 1½ ″ long
	13 No. 8 round-head wood screws, 1¼ ″ long
	12 No. 6 self-tapping pan-head sheet-metal screws, ⅝ ″ long

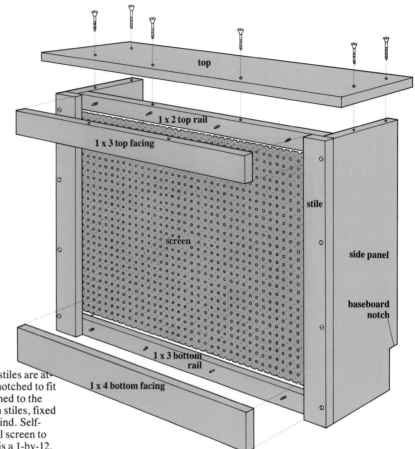

A simple radiator cover. A pair of 1-by-3 vertical stiles are attached to the front edges of 1-by-10 side panels, notched to fit over a baseboard. Top and bottom rails are attached to the backs of the stiles. Horizontal facings fit between stiles, fixed flat against the rails by screws driven in from behind. Self-tapping pan-head sheet-metal screws hold a metal screen to the backs of the stiles and facings. The top piece is a 1-by-12.

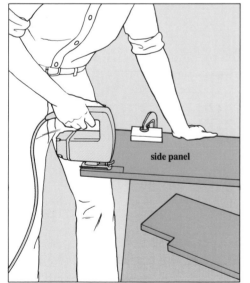

1 **Notching the side panels.** Measure the height and depth of the baseboard behind the radiator, add ⅛ inch to each measurement, and draw notches matching those dimensions on the back lower edge of each side panel. Clamp each panel in turn to a worktable, protecting the surface with a scrap of wood. Cut out the notches with a saber saw or a handsaw, sawing in from the back edge and up from the bottom so that the cuts meet at the notch's corner.

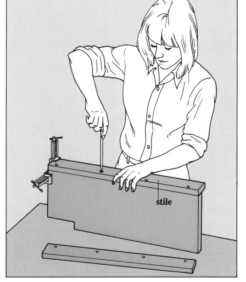

2 **Attaching stiles.** Drill four ⅜-inch counterbore holes in each 1-by-3 stile, ⅜ inch from one edge. Drill ³/₁₆-inch holes through each counterbore. Clamp a stile to the front of a side panel, as above, and mark through the holes. Unclamp the stile and drill ³/₃₂-inch pilot holes 1 inch deep at each mark. Attach the stile to the panel with glue and 1½-inch No. 8 flat-head wood screws. Repeat for the other stile and panel.

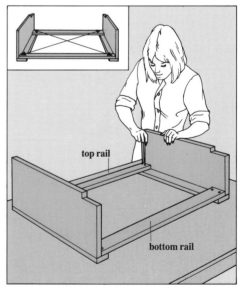

3 **Fastening rails.** Drill a ¼-inch hole through the top rail, 1 inch from each end. Drill two holes 1 inch from each end of the bottom rail. Fit the rails between the side panels (*above*). Mark through the holes, remove the rails and drill ³/₃₂-inch pilot holes ⅝ inch deep at the marks. Attach the rails with glue and 1¼-inch No. 8 round-head wood screws. Measure the assembly diagonally both ways (*inset*) to make sure it is square; tighten the screws. ▶

117

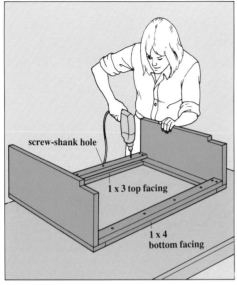

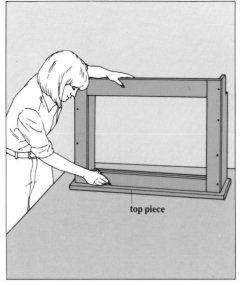

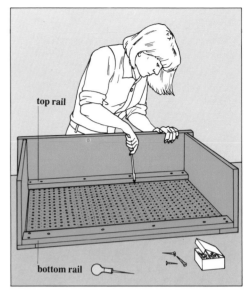

4 **Fastening facings.** Drill ³⁄₁₆-inch shank holes through each rail 3½ inches from each end; drill two more holes in between. Cut a 1-by-3 and a 1-by-4 to fit across the front of the rails. Fit the 1-by-3 beneath the top rail and the 1-by-4 beneath the bottom rail. With a ³⁄₃₂-inch bit, drill pilot holes through the shank holes ⅝ inch into the facings *(above)*. Glue the facings to the rails; secure them with 1¼-inch No. 8 round-head wood screws driven through the rails.

5 **Attaching the top.** Center the cover upside down on the 1-by-12 top piece, aligning its back edges with the back of the 1-by-12. Trace the cover *(above)*, then turn it right side up. Reposition the top, traced lines facing up. Inside the lines, drill two ³⁄₈-inch counterbore holes above each side panel's top edge. Through them, drill ³⁄₁₆-inch shank holes and ³⁄₃₂-inch pilot holes. Similarly drill two sets of holes across the front. Attach the top with 1½-inch No. 8 wood screws.

6 **Attaching the screen.** Measure inside the cover between the two side panels and the inside edges of the top and bottom rails. Subtract ¼ inch from each measurement and cut a sheet of metal screen to fit. With the radiator cover on its face, place the screen over the opening. Use an awl to punch starter holes spaced about 6 inches apart around the perimeter of the screen; drive in ⅝-inch No. 6 self-tapping pan-head sheet-metal screws.

A Paneled Cover

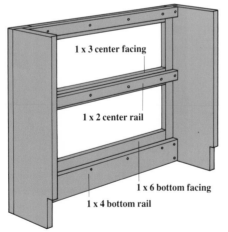

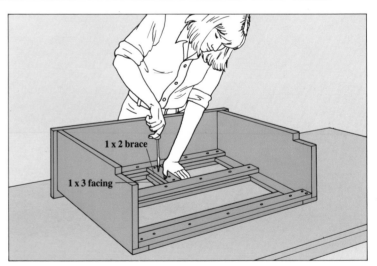

1 **Building the frame.** Start building a basic radiator cover, following Steps 1-3 on page 117, but make the bottom rail a 1-by-4 instead of a 1-by-3. Cut a 1-by-2 center rail and fasten it about a third of the distance down from the bottom of the top rail to the floor. Then follow the instructions in Step 4 *(above)* to attach a 1-by-3 top facing and a 1-by-6 bottom facing. Cut a 1-by-3 center facing and attach it similarly to the center rail, overlapping the rail's upper and lower edges equally. Attach a top as in Step 5. Measure from the bottom edge of the top rail to the top edge of the center rail and cut a 1-by-2 vertical brace to that length. Measure from the bottom edge of the top facing to the top edge of the center facing and cut a 1-by-3 vertical facing to that length.

2 **Attaching the vertical facing.** Fit the 1-by-2 vertical brace between the top and center rails at the middle of the cover, and attach it to the back of the top and center facings with 1¼-inch No. 8 round-head wood screws driven through ³⁄₁₆-inch shank holes into ³⁄₃₂-inch pilot holes. Fit the 1-by-3 vertical facing on the front of the 1-by-2 vertical brace, overlapping the 1-by-2's edges equally; attach the 1-by-3 with two 1¼-inch round-head wood screws driven through holes drilled in the back of the 1-by-2.

A Dowel-Fronted Cover

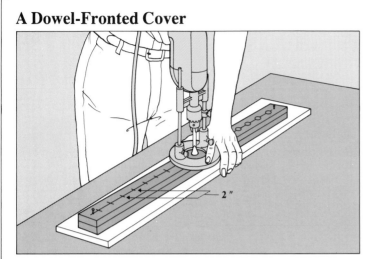

1 **Drilling dowel-frame pieces.** Measure the radiator as described in the text on page 116, but add 2 inches to the radiator's depth measurement to get the width of the side panels. Build the basic cover, following Steps 1-5 of the preceding instructions. Next, measure across the front of the cover between the inside surfaces of its side panels, and cut two 1-by-2s to that length. Place one 1-by-2 on top of the other. Draw a line lengthwise down the middle of the face of the top 1-by-2; then, starting at the center of the line and working out to the ends, make cross marks at 2-inch intervals. Align the 1-by-2s and tack them onto scrap lumber with brads. Using a drill fitted with a drill guide *(page 122)* and a ¾-inch spade bit, bore holes through the 1-by-2s at each cross mark.

2 **Fitting dowel assembly into place.** Measure inside the cover from the lower edge of the top rail to the upper edge of the bottom rail, and cut to that length enough ¾-inch dowels to fill all the pairs of holes drilled in the preceding step. Insert the ends of the dowels into the holes in one of the 1-by-2s. Then push the other 1-by-2 onto the other ends of the dowels. If necessary, tap the second 1-by-2 onto the rods with a hammer cushioned by a block of wood. Fit the assembly into the cover's opening, with the 1-by-2s wedged against the top and bottom rails. Drive fourpenny finishing nails, spaced every four inches, through the top 1-by-2 into the top rail and through the bottom 1-by-2 into the bottom rail.

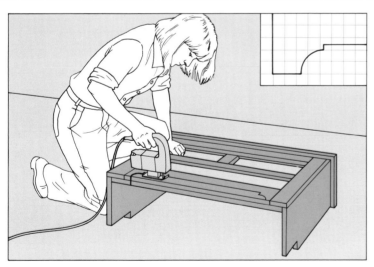

3 **Cutting out the base.** Draw a grid of 1-inch squares on a piece of lightweight cardboard and transfer the base foot pattern in the inset above to your grid, square for square. Cut out the pattern, lay it on the cover's bottom facing and trace it; flip it over and trace it again on the opposite end of the board. Join the two tracings with a horizontal pencil line, then use a saber saw to cut out the base.

4 **Attaching molding.** Following the instructions in Step 2, bottom, on page 92, cut 1⅛-inch roman ogee cap molding with mitered ends to fit across the front and sides of the cover just under the top. Attach the molding with 1-inch brads. Then cut strips of ¾-inch ogee shoe molding with mitered ends to fit the inner edges of the three openings in the cover's front; nail them in place *(above)*. Next, lay the cover face down, and cut and attach a piece of metal screen behind the two upper openings *(Step 6, opposite)*. Finally, cut a rectangle of ¼-inch plywood to fit the bottom opening, and attach it to the backs of the stiles and the bottom and center facings with ¾-inch No. 8 round-head wood screws.

Using power tools safely

Power tools ranging from saber saws to sewing machines are indispensable aids to a home decorator. If purchased wisely and handled properly, the tools on these pages will ensure professional-looking results even for the novice.

In general, inferior tools produce inferior work no matter how experienced the operator may be. When you are looking for shop tools, pass by the least expensive ones. At most hardware stores and home-improvement centers, you should be able to find relatively high-quality tools at moderate prices. Look especially for such features as heavy-duty electrical cords, permanently lubricated bearings that simplify tool maintenance, and double-insulated plastic bodies that eliminate the need for a grounded power cord with a three-prong plug. For projects that call for sewing, you need a sewing machine capable of making straight, zigzag and reverse stitches.

Just as important as buying the right tools is using the right tool for the job. A saber saw, for example, is designed for cutting curves (below); although it can make a long, straight cut through plywood, the straight cut will be cleaner and more precise if it is done with a circular saw instead (opposite). All power tools come with manufacturer's instructions for care and handling. Take the time to read the instructions, then practice with the tools before you begin a project.

Safety is as important as skill in the operation of power tools, and a few rules apply in every situation:

● Dress for the job. Avoid loose clothing, tuck in your shirt and roll up your sleeves. Tie back your hair if it is long. And wear goggles when there is a possibility that dust or shavings will fly into your eyes — for example, whenever you are sawing or drilling at eye level or overhead. Do not wear gloves when operating power tools; gloves reduce dexterity and can catch in moving parts.

● When operating a power tool, be sure to work on a stable surface; with wood projects, clamp materials to the surface whenever practical.

● Stand comfortably, do not reach any farther than you easily can, and never stand directly in front of — or directly behind — a moving saw blade.

Circular saws tend to kick back toward the operator if the blade gets jammed in the middle of a cut; this generally happens when the sawed section of a workpiece has not been supported as it ought to be to let the saw blade move freely. If the blade should bind while you are making a cut, switch the saw off immediately and support the work to open the cut.

If you are making long cuts in boards or plywood, recruit a helper to support the work for you.

● Always unplug power tools when they are not in use, and whenever you adjust or change parts.

The Saber Saw

Because the blade of a saber saw, or jig saw, as it is also known, is only about ¼ inch wide, it can be maneuvered through tight spots and intricate, curved cuts without binding or breaking. With straight cuts, the narrow blade tends to wander from a guideline. But a straightedge guide clamped to the work (opposite, bottom) will help keep such cuts on line.

Your best buy is a variable-speed saw that you can speed up along broad curves and slow down for tricky areas. Blades are sold in sets or individually. Most will cut through wood up to 2 inches thick. Blades with six teeth per inch make fast, rough cuts; blades with 10 to 14 teeth per inch cut more slowly, but also more cleanly. For fine cuts in plywood, buy taper-ground blades with 10 teeth per inch.

To ensure a smooth cut on the good face of a board or panel, work with that surface down. The saber-saw blade cuts on the upstroke, sometimes tearing slivers from the top surface of the work.

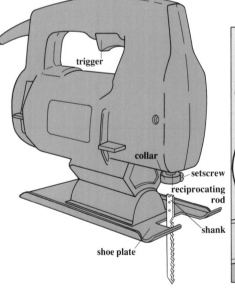

A variable-speed saber saw. A trigger in the handle lets you turn the saw on and off and regulate the speed with which it cuts. To insert a blade, loosen the setscrew in the collar on the reciprocating rod with a screwdriver or a hex wrench, depending on the saw model. Push the notched shank of the blade as far as it will go up into the hollow portion of the reciprocating rod, then retighten the setscrew to anchor the blade.

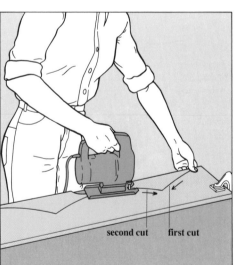

Cutting a curved pattern. Plan cuts so you will not force the blade through an impossibly tight turn; here, both cuts move toward a sharp corner. Rest the tip of the shoe plate on the wood. Start the saw, and guide the blade into the wood, swinging the back of the saw right or left as you move into curves. Do not force the blade, lest it bind or break. If you end a cut with the blade in the wood, let the blade stop before withdrawing it.

The Circular Saw

The easiest way to get wood cut to size is to have it sawed at a lumberyard. To avoid this extra expense, however, you may decide to cut the pieces yourself, using a circular saw *(right)*. The inexpensive, compact and portable circular saw, though designed for rough carpentry, will cut the pieces for many projects with reasonable accuracy.

The standard circular saw for home use has a 7¼-inch blade that will cut through lumber up to 2 inches thick; for bevels, it tilts to any angle from 45° to 90°. To saw without binding, the motor should develop at least 1½ horsepower.

A variety of blades *(right)* is available for different cutting tasks. Carbide-tipped blades, although more expensive, will outlast ordinary steel blades and save money in the long run.

In operating the saw, a firm grip is extremely important. A 7¼-inch model weighs about 10 pounds and seems heavier at arm's length, when you are cutting large panels. For the added safety of a two-handed grip, buy a saw that has two handles.

A circular saw can be guided freehand for short cuts; for longer cuts, clamp a guide to the workpiece for accuracy *(right)*. The manufactured edge of ¼-inch plywood makes a good, straight guide. Always support lumber from below; without support, the board or panel may crack. Work the saw so that its heavy motor passes over the guide if you are using one.

Many accessories for circular saws are available at hardware stores. A patented metal guide can replace the wood straightedge shown at right. Another guide simplifies rip cutting. A circular-saw table, which holds a circular saw underneath it upside down, offers a few advantages of the professional's tool — stability and accuracy — at a lower price, but with some loss of versatility.

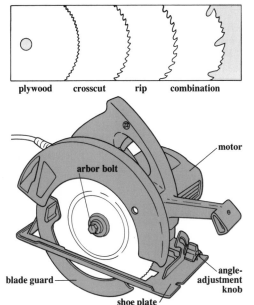

plywood   crosscut   rip   combination

Blade styles. A fine-toothed plywood blade slices through plywood without splintering it. A crosscut blade's small teeth tear smoothly across the grain; a ripping blade's larger teeth, set at a sharper angle, saw with the grain. A combination blade both rips and crosscuts, with small teeth separated by deep indentations.

The saw. Driven by a powerful motor, the blade of a circular saw cuts on the upstroke. A spring-activated guard, which slides up into the housing of the saw during operation, drops back down over the blade as the cut is finished. The angle-adjustment knob lets the shoe plate be tilted for beveled cuts. The arbor bolt, which holds the blade in place, unscrews so the blade can be changed.

(labels: motor, arbor bolt, blade guard, shoe plate, angle-adjustment knob)

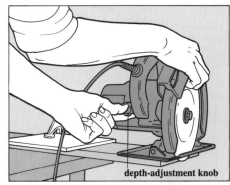

depth-adjustment knob

Adjusting blade depth. Loosen the depth-adjustment knob on the back of the saw. Lay the shoe plate flat on the wood and push up the blade guard. With one hand, hold up the guard while grasping the blade housing to support the saw body. Keeping the shoe plate flat, raise or lower the saw body — and with it the blade — until the blade is about ¼ inch below the bottom surface of the board to be cut. Retighten the depth-adjustment knob.

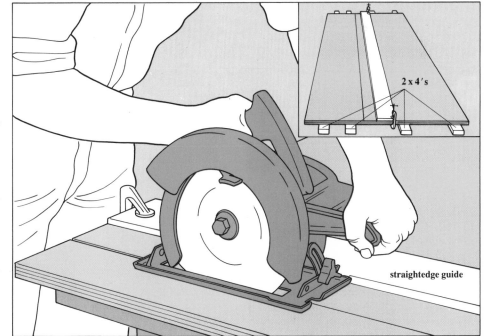

2 x 4's

straightedge guide

Sawing with a straightedge. Clamp a straightedge to the board to be cut so the blade falls just on the waste side of the cutting line. Put on goggles before sawing. To cut a large plywood panel *(inset),* rest the panel on the floor, on 2-by-4s. Holding the saw firmly, cut slowly along the straightedge. Do not force the blade — it may bind. Keep a steady grip on the saw as it clears the board, and prepare to catch its unsupported weight.

The Variable-Speed Drill

Like the saber saw, the variable-speed drill works at a variety of speeds, depending on how hard you squeeze its trigger. Small holes in wood are bored at the fastest speeds; slower speeds are better for drilling large holes in wood and for any hole in metal or masonry.

The ⅜-inch drill at right can accommodate bit shanks from ¹⁄₆₄ inch to ⅜ inch in diameter. Within that range, many different bits are available to drill holes from ¹⁄₆₄ inch to 1½ inches in diameter in wood, metal or masonry. Power drills also can hold the shanks of such accessories as buffing wheels, grinding wheels and hole saws.

The drill is often used to drill the hole for a wood screw that fastens together two boards. This task actually requires three holes: one in the bottom board to grip the screw's threads tightly, and two successively wider holes in the top board for the shank and head. You can use a separate twist bit for each hole, then broaden the top hole with a countersink bit. More simply, you can bore all three holes at once with a counterbore bit, which matches the shape of the screw's threads and shank, and has an adjustable head that bores, or counterbores, a recess for the screw-

head. Avoid cheap counterbore bits: They tend to clog.

Spade bits bore holes up to 1½ inches in diameter; because these bits tend to wobble, use of a drill guide is advisable. The model below, at right, will fit any drill with a threaded shaft.

Masonry bits, with closely spaced, carbide-tipped edges, grind slowly through brick, concrete and tile, which would quickly dull an ordinary twist bit.

Masonry and spade bits are most often sold singly; countersinks are sold in only one size. Counterbore and twist bits are sold singly and in sets that include the most frequently used sizes.

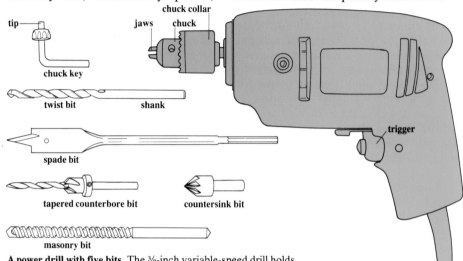

A power drill with five bits. The ⅜-inch variable-speed drill holds twist, spade, counterbore, countersink and masonry bits with shanks up to ⅜ inch in diameter. To insert a bit, turn the chuck collar to open the jaws, push the bit shank between the jaws and tighten the collar by hand until the jaws grip the shank. Then push the tip of the chuck key into one of the three holes in the chuck, and twist the key handle. To change bits, loosen the collar with the chuck key before turning it by hand.

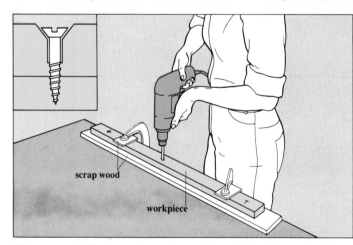

Using a power drill. Clamp the work to a table and indent the wood at the starting point with an awl. To govern a hole's depth, wrap tape around the bit at the required distance from the tip. Set the bit in the dent, squeeze the trigger and push the drill straight down with steady, moderate pressure. To drill holes for a wood screw (inset), use a tapered counterbore bit (above). Or drill two holes of increasing size, a narrow one in the bottom piece for the screw's threads and a wide one in the top for the shank. Widen the hole's mouth with a countersink bit if it will be puttied, or use a third twist bit if it will be plugged with a short dowel.

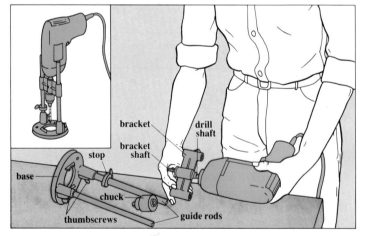

Attaching a drill guide. Remove the drill's chuck. (Most unscrew from the shaft of the drill, but check the manufacturer's instructions.) Twist the guide bracket onto the drill shaft; screw the chuck onto the bracket's shaft. Slip the guide rods through their holes in the bracket, loosen the thumbscrews on the base, set the ends of the rods flush with the bottom of the base, and tighten the screws; this procedure ensures that the holes drilled are perpendicular to the work surface when the drill guide is upright (inset). If you want to drill to a certain depth, position the stop on the guide rod after you have inserted a bit in the chuck.

The Sewing Machine

The sewing machine is one of the easiest home tools to use and maintain. A good machine is virtually trouble-free mechanically and needs only a light oiling every three or four operating hours.

Threading the machine properly is essential; the owner's manual will tell you how. Although every model threads somewhat differently, there are always two threads, an upper thread from the spool and a lower thread wound around the bobbin (*right*). The tension on the upper thread is adjusted with a knob.

Generally, pair synthetic thread with synthetic fabric, and natural with natural, so that, in cleaning, fabric and thread shrink at the same rate. You may also use dual-duty thread, a cotton-covered polyester that works well with almost all fabrics. Use size 50 thread and a size 14 needle for most fabrics, and a heavier thread and a size 16 needle for thick fabrics, such as canvas.

The standard number of stitches per inch for a seam is 12 to 15; use more if very strong seams are needed.

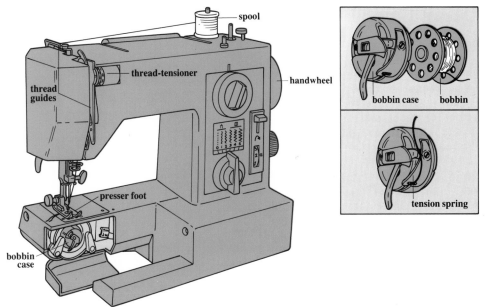

The versatile sewing machine. Every sewing machine has a set of thread guides that take the thread from the spool, through an adjustable thread-tensioner and down to the needle. A second thread is wound around a lower spool called the bobbin (*top inset*) and slipped underneath a tension spring (*bottom inset*) on the bobbin case.

Dials on the machine set the type, length and direction of a stitch. The presser foot, a ski-shaped clamp that holds the fabric flat, comes in a variety of configurations for special stitches. The feed dog, a toothed plate below the presser foot, advances the fabric automatically. The handwheel turns the mechanism to start the first stitch.

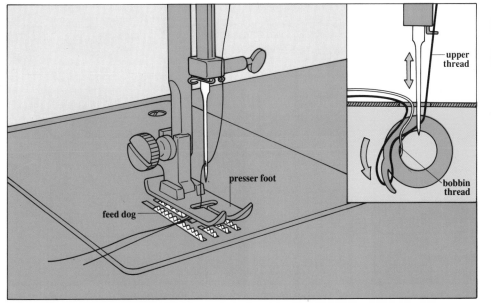

Preparing to sew. After threading the machine, lower the presser foot, grasp the end of the upper thread and turn the handwheel slowly toward yourself. As you do this, the upper thread will tighten around the bobbin thread (*inset*) and pull it up in a loop. Raise the presser foot and pull out the end of the bobbin thread from the loop. Draw out both threads 3 or 4 inches and pull the ends together to the rear of the presser foot.

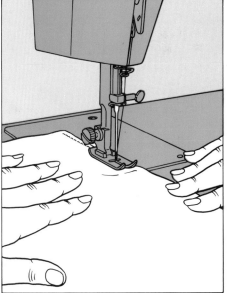

Sewing the fabric. Position the fabric under the needle. Lower the presser foot, turn on the machine, and guide the fabric as the feed dog pulls it forward. When you finish sewing, set the machine in reverse and backstitch over the last few stitches for reinforcement. Then raise the presser foot, pull out the fabric and cut both threads.

The Right Brush for the Job

Several types of brushes are employed in the wall-painting projects shown in this volume. Choosing the correct brush for the job *(right)* and giving it careful maintenance *(below)* will pay off both in the ease of applying the finish and in the quality of the results.

Matching the type of brush bristles to the type of paint you will be using is a primary consideration. Natural bristles, also called China bristles, are preferred for alkyd paints. These resilient bristles have natural split ends that enable them to pick up more paint than smooth hairs would. But because natural bristles swell in contact with water, nylon or polyester bristles are better for water-based or latex paints. Check the ends of synthetic bristles to be sure they have been flagged — frayed to mimic natural bristles.

For decorative work, sable bristles are unrivaled because of their suppleness. However, in the large-size artist's brushes *(far right)*, less expensive China bristles may be used.

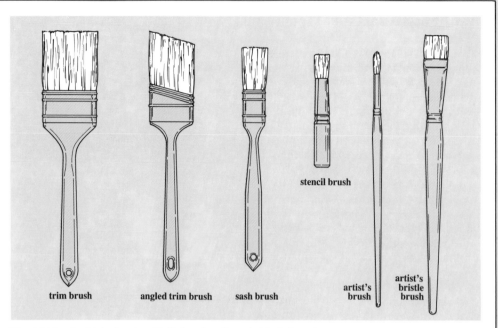

trim brush   angled trim brush   sash brush   stencil brush   artist's brush   artist's bristle brush

The right brush. A trim brush, with its long handle and chisel-shaped working end, is generally used in wall painting for techniques that require precise edges or lines. A trim brush with angled bristles lets you work in hard-to-reach wall areas. Use a slender sash brush to paint narrow surfaces such as window frames. Brushes specially designed for stenciling are available in many sizes: Choose one proportional to your design. Artist's brushes handle the intricate details of jobs such as painting the simulated wall molding on page 95.

1 **Cleaning a brush.** After each job, wash the brush thoroughly in the solvent recommended by the finish manufacturer by first pouring at least an inch of solvent into a shallow container. Put on rubber gloves, then dip the brush's bristles into the solvent and swirl them back and forth. Remove excess solvent by squeezing the bristles between your thumb and fingers. Keep swirling and squeezing until the bristles look clean, changing the solvent whenever it becomes heavily clouded. Wash the brush with warm water and mild soap until the lather is clean and white, then rinse the brush well. Blot the brush dry with a clean, absorbent rag.

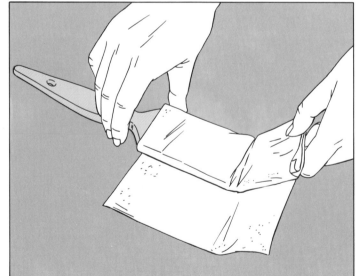

2 **Wrapping the brush for storage.** Lay the bristles and body of the brush across one end of a long strip of brown wrapping paper. The paper should extend several inches beyond the bristle tips. Fold the paper over the brush, then roll the brush and paper until the brush is encased in three or four layers of paper. Fold the end of the paper up over the bristles, being careful not to bend the bristle tips; crease the paper so it holds its position. Finish wrapping the paper around the brush and secure it with tape or a rubber band. Store the brush on a flat surface or hang it from the hole in its handle.

Basic Fasteners

Objects attached to your walls are only as secure as the fasteners that hold them in place. The concealed framework of wall studs and ceiling joists provides firm anchorage; a method for locating a stud or joist is shown on page 19.

If the studs or joists are conveniently located, nails or wood screws are the fasteners of choice. Where no framing members exist, light loads may be attached with expanding anchors that grip the edges of holes drilled into wallboard or plaster. For heavier loads you need toggle bolts, which cling to a wall or ceiling by squeezing from both sides *(below)*.

Other expanding anchors are available for masonry walls, which can bear a load at any point. If the surface of a masonry wall is exposed and you have a choice, avoid the joints since mortar is comparatively soft and crumbly.

The partition walls of many apartment buildings have been built with metal studs. Self-tapping screws are recommended for this type of construction.

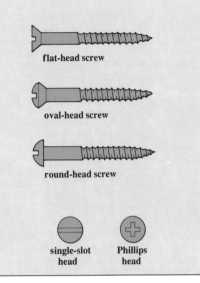

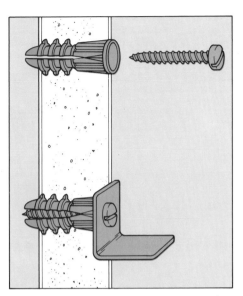

Wood screws. Flat-head screws are countersunk flush with the surface or hidden beneath plugs or putty. Round and oval heads can be left exposed. Heads have one slot or, for a Phillips ™ screwdriver, two crossed slots. Phillips heads are less likely to rip under turning pressure. Screw-shaft diameters are denoted by gauge numbers: The higher the number, the larger the diameter.

Anchor. The sides of an anchor press out to gain a tight grip in masonry, wallboard or plaster when a matching-size screw is driven into it. A plastic anchor *(above)*, sufficient for light loads, can be used with a wood screw or a self-tapping screw *(shown)*. Heavier weights need lead anchors. With either type, tap the anchor into a hole drilled to fit it snugly. (In wallboard, as here, the anchor and screw should be long enough to extend through it.) Insert the screw through the object to be hung, and drive it into the anchor.

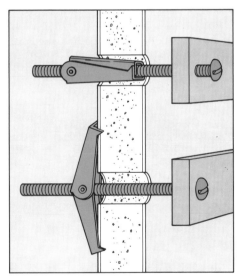

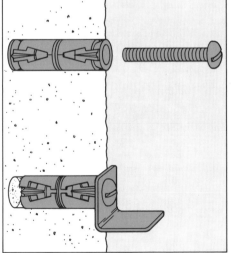

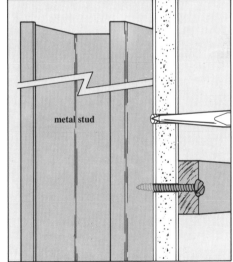

Toggle bolt. A toggle bolt must be long enough for its wings to spring open and grip the inside of a hollow wall. Drill a hole large enough for the folded wings to pass through, but do not push them in at this stage. Unscrew the wings from the bolt, slip the bolt through the object to be hung, and replace the wings. Then push the bolt through the wall; when the wings pop open, the bolt will feel loose in the hole. Pull the device back so that the wings will bite into the inside of the wall as you tighten the bolt.

Expansion shield. This metal device with interior threads is used with a matching machine screw to hold a load on masonry or a thick plaster wall. Drill a hole that will hold the shield snugly, and tap the shield into it. Make sure the screw is long enough to extend through the hanger of the object being hung and the length of the shield. As you tighten the screw, wedges in the shield will be pulled toward the middle, pushing the cylinder sides hard against the masonry or plaster.

Self-tapping screw. This sort of screw is used to attach weights to metal studs. Drill a small hole in the wallboard to the face of the stud. Make a starter dent in the stud with a center punch and a hammer. Then use a twist bit to drill a pilot hole half the diameter of the screw through the thin metal. Insert the screw through the object you are hanging, and drive it into the stud; the screw should be long enough to reach about ½ inch beyond the face of the stud.

Acknowledgments

The index for this book was prepared by Louise Hedberg. The editors are particularly indebted to Stan Warshaw, U.S. School of Professional Paperhanging, Inc., Rutland, Vermont, and Magenta Yglesias, ASID, Washington, D.C. For their help in the preparation of this volume, the editors also wish to thank the following: Julie Avery, Sidney Paint Center, Sidney, New York; Longine Beck, Household Products Division, 3M, St. Paul, Minnesota; Andrea Bodenburg, Gruner und Jahr, Hamburg; Wulf Brackrock, Hamburg; Royal A. Brown, Vienna, Virginia; Marika Carniti, Rome; Barry Digwood, Crown Decorative Products Ltd., Darwen, Lancashire, England; George Evans, Evans Custom Drapery, Chevy Chase, Maryland; Mr. and Mrs. James W. Frierson, Alexandria, Virginia; Monika Gay, Gruner und Jahr, Hamburg; Isidoro Genovese, Rome; Richard Hall, Wallcovering Information Bureau, Springfield, New Jersey; Peter Hisey, Publishing Dynamics, Inc., Stamford, Connecticut; Marion Kaufmann, Jahreszeiten Verlag, Hamburg; Pat Kennedy, Pat Kennedy Drapery Installation, Takoma Park, Maryland; Whitney Lewis, Bentley Brothers, Louisville, Kentucky; Massimo Listri, Florence, Italy; Kathleen Middleton, Torpedo Factory Art Center, Alexandria, Virginia; Gene Nelson, Georgia-Pacific Corporation, Atlanta, Georgia; Lucinda Newton, Washington, D.C.; Giovanni Patrini, Milan; Richard Paul, "Plaisir de la Maison," Paris; Giovanna Piemonti, Rome; Penne Poole, Penne Poole Interior Design, Inc., Washington, D.C.; James Prett, Industrial Tape Division, 3M, St. Paul, Minnesota; Guy De Vendeuvre, Paris; Elke Wall, Granny's Place, Alexandria, Virginia; Lynn Addison Yorke, Hyattsville, Maryland.

Picture Credits

The sources for the photographs in this book are listed below, followed by the sources for the illustrations. Credits from left to right on a single page or a two-page spread are separated by semicolons; credits from top to bottom are separated by dashes.

Photographs: **Cover:** Larry Sherer, photographer / location, courtesy Mr. and Mrs. Thomas L. Higginson Jr. / design by Augusta Moravec Interiors, Bethesda, Maryland. **2, 3:** Aldo Ballo, photographer, Milan / design by Flavio Albanese, Vicenza. **4, 5:** Pascal Hinous, photographer, from Agence TOP, Paris / painting by Guy De Vendeuvre. **6, 7:** Emmett Bright, photographer / design by Angela Ziffer, Rome; © Wulf Brackrock, photographer, Hamburg. **8:** © 1985 Paul Warchol, photographer / Garrison-Donaldson Architects, New York. **9:** © 1984 Paul Warchol, photographer / design by Booth/Hansen & Associates, Chicago, Illinois. **10, 11:** Maris/Semel, photographers / design by Norman Jaffe, architect, Bridgehampton, New York. **25:** Larry Sherer, photographer. **28, 29:** Michael Latil, photographer. **38:** Michael Latil, photographer / table setting, except spoons, courtesy Iberian Imports, Alexandria, Virginia. **42, 43:** Peter Harholdt, photographer / table, courtesy Marquise Jewelers, Ltd. of Olde Towne, Alexandria, Virginia / lamp, courtesy Parr Excellence Carpet and Interior Design, Alexandria, Virginia. **44-48:** Peter Harholdt, photographer. **50:** Chuck Ashley, photographer, courtesy *Creative Ideas for Living* / styling by Helen Heitkamp / stencil design by Julia Salles Hass, execution by Liddie Schmidt and Linda Kilgore, Tiburon, California. **66, 67:** Michael Latil, photographer. **68:** Motif Designs — courtesy Imperial Wallcoverings; Michael Latil, photographer. **69:** Courtesy Charles Barone, Inc.; Robert Grant, photographer, courtesy Motif Designs. **72:** Michael Latil, photographer, courtesy of and design by Magenta Yglesias, ASID, Washington, D.C. / tablecloth and napkins, courtesy Walpole's, Inc., Chevy Chase, Maryland. **80, 81:** Courtesy Georgia-Pacific Corporation. **95:** Michael Latil, photographer / design and execution by Nancy T. Baker, Alexandria, Virginia, and Cindy B. Fitch, Washington, D.C. **100:** Dan Cunningham, photographer / rug, courtesy the Kellogg Collection, Washington, D.C. / antiques, courtesy Frances Simmons Antiques and Accessories, Alexandria, Virginia. **108:** Michael Latil, photographer. **114:** Michael Latil, photographer / rug, courtesy the Kellogg Collection, Washington, D.C. — Michael Latil, photographer.

Illustrations: **16-19:** Drawings by George Bell, inked by Eduino J. Pereira. **20-23:** Drawings by Jack Arthur, inked by Adisai Hemintranont from Sai Graphis. **26:** Art by Matt McMullen. **30-37:** Drawings by Fred Holz, inked by Steve Turner. **39-41:** Drawings by Fred Holz, inked by Eduino J. Pereira. **44, 45:** Drawings by George Bell, inked by Walter Hilmers Jr. from HJ Commercial Art. **46-49:** Drawings by George Bell, inked by Walter Hilmers Jr. from HJ Commercial Art. Background renderings by Nancy Baker. **51-55:** Drawings by Fred Holz, inked by Walter Hilmers Jr. from HJ Commercial Art. **56-65:** Drawings by George Bell, inked by George Bell. **69:** Drawings by Fred Holz, inked by Elsie J. Hennig. **70, 71:** Drawings by Fred Holz, inked by Arezou Katoozian Hennessy. **73-77:** Drawings by William J. Hennessy Jr., inked by Frederic F. Bigio from B-C Graphics. **78, 79:** Drawings by Roger Essley, inked by Arezou Katoozian Hennessy. **82, 83:** Drawings by Fred Holz, inked by Elsie J. Hennig. **86-93:** Drawings by Greg DeSantis, inked by Walter Hilmers Jr. from HJ Commercial Art. **94:** Drawings by George Bell, inked by Elsie J. Hennig. **96-99:** Drawings by Jack Arthur, inked by Elsie J. Hennig. **101-107:** Drawings by Fred Holz, inked by Walter Hilmers Jr. from HJ Commercial Art. **109-113:** Drawings by William J. Hennessy Jr., inked by Arezou Katoozian Hennessy. **115:** Drawings by Roger Essley, inked by Arezou Katoozian Hennessy. **116-119:** Drawings by Jack Arthur, inked by John Massey. **120-122:** Drawings by Roger Essley, inked by Adisai Hemintranont from Sai Graphis. **123:** Drawings by Roger Essley, inked by Frederic F. Bigio from B-C Graphics. **124:** Drawing by William J. Hennessy Jr., inked by Walter Hilmers Jr. from HJ Commercial Art — drawings by William J. Hennessy Jr., inked by Arezou Katoozian Hennessy. **125:** Drawings by Fred Holz, inked by Walter Hilmers Jr. from HJ Commercial Art.

Index/Glossary

Time-Life Books Inc. offers a wide range of fine recordings, including a *Big Bands* series. For subscription information, call 1-800-621-7026, or write TIME-LIFE MUSIC, Time & Life Building, Chicago, Illinois 60611.